Winning Elections:

A Handbook in Participatory Politics

Winning Elections:

A Handbook in Participatory Politics

Dick Simpson

THE SWALLOW PRESS INC.
CHICAGO

Printed in United States of America

Published by
The Swallow Press Incorporated
1139 S. Wabash Avenue
Chicago, Illinois 60605

ISBN (cloth) 0-8040-0541-9
ISBN (paper) 0-8040-0542-7
LIBRARY OF CONGRESS CATALOG NO. 78-171874

This book is printed on 100% recycled paper.

I wish gratefully to acknowledge that much of what I know about participatory politics I learned in some dozen campaigns working with leaders like John Kearney, Sherwin Swartz and Robert Houston. Further, had Eugene McCarthy not dared to run for President in 1968, I might never have become involved. But, most of all, had hundreds of volunteers not continually renewed my faith by their sacrifices, I would not have maintained so steadfastly my own commitment.

I owe a special debt to Professors George Beam and Susan Markle of the University of Illinois at Chicago Circle for critically reading the first draft of this book. Chapter IV was carefully corrected and greatly improved by Don Rose, editor of *Hyde Park-Kenwood Voices*. Jim Chapman, Executive Director of the Independent Precinct Organization, suggested specific elaborations and the proper emphasis for the chapters on campaign structure and precinct work.

My wife, Mary Scott, and the editors at Swallow Press were able to improve the early drafts to an amazing degree. Despite all of this help, I have no doubt that *Winning Elections* still has many errors of syntax, fact and analysis. For these I take full responsibility. I hope, nonetheless, that this handbook may help many people to better understand the great potential of participatory politics.

For the members of IPO and all practitioners of participatory politics

I know no safe depository of the ultimate powers of the society but the people themselves; and if we think them not enlightened enough to exercise their control with a wholesome discretion, the remedy is not to take it from them, but to inform their discretion.

THOMAS JEFFERSON
Letter to William Charles Jarvis
September 28, 1820

Organize the whole state, so that every Whig can be brought to the polls . . . divide the county into small districts and appoint in each a sub-committee . . . make a perfect list of voters and ascertain with certainty for whom they will vote . . . and on election day see that every Whig is brought to the polls.

ABRAHAM LINCOLN
Illinois State Register
February 21, 1840

Contents

Chapter I
The Beginning

In 1968 I was campaign manager in Illinois' 9th Congressional District and later, state campaign manager for Eugene McCarthy's bid for the Presidency. In the primary in the 9th Congressional District, McCarthy delegates received only twenty percent of the vote; in the entire state we elected only two of our twenty-two candidates. As a direct result of losing campaigns such as these, particularly in non-primary states, we lost the nomination at the Democratic National Convention. Many people, disappointed or bitter about their experiences in 1968, decided to abandon electoral politics as a means of bringing change in the United States.

For myself, McCarthy's defeat was a profound learning experience. I still believed that our goal of revitalizing American politics was sound, but that we had not known enough about campaigning in 1968. In the McCarthy campaign our energies were directed toward change at the top of the power structure, but there are other ways of winning elections and other bases of power in this country. Instead of starting at the top, it now seemed that a strong, determined reform movement could be built from the bottom, in local communities throughout the nation. Along with others who shared this belief, I resolved to learn what it meant to develop such a grass-roots constituency.

This book is a distillation of our successes and failures over the last three years. It is a continuation of strategy meetings in a dozen local Chicago campaigns and of many seminars in practical politics.

While this book may provide information and self-confidence, the commitment to elect honest, responsive political leaders instead of political hacks, to open up the political process rather than keep it a closed game for insiders — this commitment you must develop on your own. If you have it, the handbook can suggest how to translate your abstract beliefs into positive action. If you lack commitment, no rules or advice can help you find it. Practitioners of effective participatory politics must begin with a strong faith that people can and should have an important voice in governing themselves.

Winning Elections is about new politics, or more precisely, participatory politics, in which citizens find candidates they want to elect to office and then, with or without party support, put together a voluntary campaign that will win. Participatory politics differs from old politics because it focuses upon issues critical to constituents, upon candidates who are free from the control of party bosses, and upon volunteers rather than patronage precinct captains or expensive public relations. Not only will the skills of organizing participatory campaigns prove useful to you as an individual, but they can affect the political history of your district. The most limited commodity in any campaign are sophisticated political leaders who know *what* to do, *why* they are doing it, *when* to begin, and *how* to obtain maximum results. As you work in campaigns, you will begin to understand better the principles presented here. And by the end of several campaigns, you will become one of the much-needed skilled political workers and able to write your own textbook on participatory politics. To the extent that you learn the lessons in *Winning Elections* and gain practical political experience, you are making more sweeping reforms possible.

Personal decisions

This handbook emphasizes many of the mechanical and generalized aspects of running a winning campaign. But a campaign is composed of human beings, not machines; campaign issues are concrete, not abstract; and campaigns take their own character from particular personalities and events. A campaign is finally won or lost by specific decisions made by specific individuals. Put another way, a campaign is composed of choices — the choice by a candidate to run; choices by leaders and participants to work; the decision to take public stands on some issues while ignoring others; the selection of a campaign theme and basic principles on which the candidate will base his appeal to the electorate; and the final decision by each voter whether or not to vote and for whom. Each choice has consequences for both the person making the decision and for the outcome of the election. Because of their importance to a fuller understanding of elections, this introductory chapter shall focus on the personal decisions which breathe life into an otherwise mechanical process, making each campaign unique.

Everyone in the campaign makes a decision to devote time, talent, and money to the campaign. For the candidate and key campaign leaders, this decision is of a different magnitude than that required of other volunteers, workers, and contributors. Not only do the candidate and key leaders risk more of their time and fortune, they risk more of themselves. At coffees and through personal contacts, ordinary citizens are asked to reaffirm the campaign and to provide the support necessary for victory, but it is the candidate and campaign leaders who must launch the campaign. It is the candidate who risks his name, who must pay debts incurred in the campaign, who is ridiculed and abused by the opposition. Most of all, it is the candidate who asks people to help *him* — to elect *him* to office. A proud man may find it distressing to stand in front of stores shaking hands or to go to friends and associates asking for money for himself. Yet the candidate is his own best fund raiser and worker. He or she has to learn to ask people to support him if one is to run a good campaign. For many candidates this is the most painful lesson of the campaign.

Similarly, no candidate is really drafted. Some friends or citizen groups may ask him if he is interested in running, but, at some point, the candidate must decide that he *is* running and begin to seek the help and support necessary to win. If he decides to run, the campaign is launched. If he refuses or hesitates, his campaign is lost and someone else steps forward. The decision of one person — the candidate — to risk all on the bid for public office is the most important decision of the campaign and one that only the candidate can make.

There are so many concrete reasons not to run — it will mean so much time lost from the family; it may take you away from the profession that you have spent years building; and it will cost a lot of money. The positive reasons to run seem terribly abstract — your election will give the community a strong representative and spokesman; it will make government more efficient; and some reform legislation can be introduced. But once the decision to go ahead is made, the others as to how to mount the most effective campaign are much simpler.

Key campaign personnel also face difficult decisions. A staff member must decide to take a leave of absence or interrupt his vocation in order to work full time. Like the candidate, staff must expect endless hours of work and separation from their families. They must struggle with the questions of whether or not they can do the job and whether they are willing to make the necessary sacrifices. It is one thing to support a candidate, to give a few hours or to donate a few dollars to the campaign, but serving as a campaign leader requires dedication and, usually, personal commitment to the candidate.

The sacrifice required of others is in many ways the greatest burden a candidate undertakes. That his campaign will disrupt many people's lives, will require their contributions of work and money places on him the responsibility of conducting the campaign in a fashion that makes it worth these sacrifices — and of continuing even though he may sometimes wish to back out.

The candidate and the people who take on the key leadership positions undertake a collective action with great consequences both for themselves and for their community. Once the decisions to run and to support a candidate are made, the campaign leaders must still decide upon a general theme and take positive actions which will symbolize to the press and to the community what the campaign is all about. In my own campaign, my proposal of a citizen ordinance to limit the power of the mayor in school board appointments made it clear that I would not be a "rubber stamp" alderman. Such actions on the part of a candidate help create the enthusiasm and support necessary to win. Thus, the candidate and his supporters must find creative ways of dramatizing the campaign. Unless they do, neither coffees nor precinct work is likely to be sufficient. Existential choices, controversial issues, bold action — these are some of the human stuff of campaigns. The campaign structure, the hard work in the precincts provide a base, but good campaigns embody issues and actions which cannot be completely planned in advance.

Participatory Politics

What difference will it make if you, and other readers like you, learn the principles of participatory politics? I believe that it could make the difference between the type of political future we want and the future we fear. As Martin Luther King was so fond of telling us, "There is nothing so powerful as an idea whose time has come." The time for a new politics is at hand.

Participatory politics is "new" in several ways. It requires new citizens, new leaders, and a different relationship between them than presently exists. Participatory politics requires that many citizens be willing to make personal sacrifices to elect the best of themselves to public office, to support and criticize those officials once elected, and to make sure that public officials know citizen opinions on important policy questions. More than this, it means that citizens must take the responsibility to do some things for themselves, rather than depending upon Big Government to take care of them. Just as the city government should not be expected to sweep the sidewalks in front of private homes or stores, so a downtown Board of Education should not be allowed to make neighborhood school decisions which can better be determined by the citizens of the local community.

As for the leaders, participatory politics requires elected officials who have a vision of how best to maximize the *human* possibilities of political institutions. They must be people of conscience, able to speak out clearly on important moral questions in order to help guide public opinion. They must be just men and women who will not use their power to tyrannize citizens. And most of all, they must truly be "of the people" — representatives who will listen to the complaints and suggestions of average citizens in order to better articulate these ideas and to shape them into effective government programs.

The long range aim of participatory politics is a relationship between leader and constituency based on mutual trust. Both the citizen and his elected representative must *trust* the ability of the people to know (or at least to recognize when it is articulated for them) just what their problems are and how they can be solved. And the elected representative must himself be trustworthy. He cannot afford to be personally threatened by every demand for change presented him by his constituents; rather, he must be able to absorb these articulated needs and lead in giving them institutional form.

Citizens deserve the government they create and, for that matter, leaders deserve the constituencies *they* create. Participatory politics strikes a balance between bold but responsive political leaders; critical but supportive citizens; representative democracy and direct citizen action. The possibility of creating this new politics in America is here. What is needed are dedicated men and women who know not only what to say, but how to act effectively at the right moment to alter political history.

If you do not believe that a few people can change history, let me tell you of the last few years in Chicago. Independent politics has existed in Chicago since the 1940s, and reform movements of one type or another have come and gone during the last century. But until the last few years, independent politics was mostly confined to a few wards on the south side of Chicago, principally in the Hyde Park area around the University of Chicago. In 1968 new politics was given a tremendous boost through the campaigns of Eugene McCarthy and Robert Kennedy. In the end, we failed. We did not elect enough independent delegates to the Democratic National Convention, get the platform we advocated, or nominate these candidates for president of the United States. But many of us active in those campaigns learned from our failures.

Chicago is the most machine-controlled city in our nation. Some ghetto wards still produce from eighty to ninety per cent of their votes unfailingly for the Chicago Democratic Party. In 1961 there was only one independent serving in the City Council, only a handful of independent-minded state legislators, and no Chicago Congressmen who were free of machine control. One man, Mayor Daley, was boss, and within the limits of the law (and he made many of the laws), his decisions were carried out without question. If we in Chicago could make a dent, if we could topple this machine, it would be a signal of new possibilities for the nation.

The changes began with discussions of the 1968 campaigns. It began with a little group of ten people. It began when each of the ten contributed twenty-five dollars so that we could open a headquarters. It began with an open meeting, principally of former McCarthy workers, to decide who we would work for in fall of 1968 and where we would go from there. It began when we created a new organization called the Independent Precinct Organization in three north side wards, an organization which has now expanded to encompass eight wards.

In November 1968 independents on the north side of Chicago worked for five candidates in the general election — three Democrats and two Republicans who were running for offices ranging from State Senate to U.S. Senate. Only two of these candidates were elected, but we were able to produce a marked tendency for split-ticket voting (voting for both Democrats and Republicans rather than only for the candidates of a single party) in those precincts where we worked. A few months later in February and March 1969 we worked hard for two independent aldermanic candidates. Bill Singer was elected alderman of the 44th Ward in a very tough campaign and John Stevens, a Black running in a sixty percent white ward, missed forcing a run-off election with the white machine candidate by only 742 votes. Later in 1969, both independents and the regular Democratic organization endorsed and elected Mrs. Dawn Clark Netsch as delegate to the Illinois Constitutional Convention, while in the neighboring district we were able to elect Independent Bernard Weisberg despite strong machine opposition. In 1970 we followed up the Weisberg victory by electing Independent Democrat Dr. Bruce Douglas as state representative. Also in 1970 and 1971 we carried the north side wards in favor of ratification of the new state constitution, in favor of a separate constitutional provision for merit-selection of judges, and against a proposal for an elected, but highly centralized school board. Finally, in 1971 Alderman Bill Singer was reelected by a landslide vote, and I was elected in an adjacent ward which had been specially gerrymandered to make an independent victory impossible.

In the last three years there has been a basic transformation of politics on the north side of Chicago and a consequent change in Chicago politics generally. Prior to 1968 no independent could be elected on the north side without party support, but, since then, independent electoral victories have become more and more frequent. The Chicago Democratic machine responded at first by firing precinct captains who lost their precincts and retiring ward committeemen. Then they began to slate younger and more able candidates. But because their candidates could not break free of party domination on key issues, they still lost frequently.

Electoral victories have also resulted in policy changes and vigorous issue campaigns by community and citywide organizations. Thus, Chicago now has new pollution ordinances. The particular blight in north side communities caused by shoddily constructed four-story buildings with no sideyards, little parking, polished facades, and relatively high rents has been banned. Our new state constitution has an outstanding Bill of Rights and many good articles drafted by independent delegates. The state legislature has adopted better minority group legislation and has come close to passing new welfare legislation and resolutions aiming to end the war in Vietnam. Most strikingly, there are, for the first time in many years, enough independents in Mayor Daley's City Council to form an effective block of Minority Aldermen who not only raise issues but who offer alternative proposals to major city government policies. For a community which began without any voice in government three years ago these developments represent a big step forward.

The Next Step

As Feiffer's cartoon points out so well, the alternatives offered in American politics today are either anarchy or repression. Those who would support a positive alternative of peace and an end to poverty and racism are usually ignored. The only way in which we shall get such positive goals accepted and implemented is to reform the entire political system so that peace and justice, equality and effective citizen participation become the primary goals. To do that we must see that leaders who support these goals are elected to office and, even more important, that a large constituency is developed not only to support these leaders but constantly to pressure for maximization of these ends.

Instituting new values, electing new leaders, evolving new procedures of greater participation, and developing a constituency of conscience can certainly be pursued at the national level, as the 1968 Presidential campaigns clearly demonstrated. Ultimately, however, the success of such strategies depends upon the creation of an informed constituency and capable leaders in local communities.

Our Federal Constitution was created, not only from our experience with the short-comings of the Articles of Confederation, but, more importantly, from the experiences of government in the thirteen colonies before the revolution and from the efforts to draft new constitutions for each of the states after the revolution. It was in these colonies and states that the wisdom of separating the powers of government into the executive, legislative and judicial departments, of guaranteeing certain rights, of writing a constitution at all, and of electing representatives was first tested.

From the history of the Federal Constitution we today can learn an important lesson. If we wish to make our political system more participatory, we must begin by making changes in our local communities. If we can't elect a qualified man to the City Council or State Legislature, we should not expect to elect a President and a favorable Congress. If we can't end housing segregation in our towns and cities, we should not expect to be able to alter fundamentally American foreign policy. If we are unable to defeat political parties in local contests, we cannot hope to reform them from the top. For these reasons this handbook of participatory politics focuses on how to mobilize citizens in local communities to win elections. Based upon the success of local campaigns and the trained leadership developed in local communities around the country, we will have a foundation for a national participatory politics.

This handbook attempts not only to collect the kind of information that makes for political expertise among practitioners of participatory politics, but to present this information in a way that encourages maximum learning in the briefest period of time. It may, of course, be read by itself as an introduction to innovative political campaigning. It may also be used in conjunction with the film *By the People* on the election of Bernard Weisberg as an independent delegate to the Illinois Constitutional Convention,[1] or it may be used in special training workshops (see Appendix 1).

Politics is hardly an exact science. In fact, this handbook may prove as interesting to my fellow political scientists as to campaign workers. For the last several decades we have tended to divorce political science from real politics to such an extent that the profession has little to offer in the way of advice and only a limited understanding of political activities such as campaigning. Nonetheless, I do believe that this handbook, because it is based on first-hand experiences, will equip you to run a good campaign. If I have drawn heavily on Chicago politics for my examples, it is to show that if independents have been able to win against the entrenched Democratic machine in this city, others using the same techniques should have little difficulty winning their battles elsewhere.

I hope constantly to improve both the information provided and the format of this handbook so that those who use it may become more and more effective in their efforts to nurture participatory politics in various locales. Your suggestions and reports of your own campaign experiences will help me to update and improve the handbook for future campaigners. At this stage, however, consider this book as if it were a long personal letter or a talk before a seminar of the several dozen of you who are ready to introduce or to strengthen participatory politics in your community. I share with you some of what has been learned in tough political campaigns of the last three years in which we beat the Chicago Democratic Machine, and in which I played a variety of roles ranging from precinct worker to successful candidate.

Chapter II
Choosing Up Sides

If politics in America is to be reformed, it must begin with you fighting campaigns in your own community and winning your own victories. It will not be easy. But you will find that many of your neighbors, co-workers, and people you have met only casually feel the same way you do. They are waiting for someone to take the first step—to offer viable candidates and proposals for new government policies. As the journey of a thousand miles begins with a single step, major political reform begins when a single citizen commits himself to winning elections, to changing public policies, and to opening up the political process.

Getting into politics

Politics is such a dirty business! You're too good to get involved with all those liars and cheats! In a position of responsibility like yours you just can't afford the time. And you don't know anything about politics, anyway.

Friends and family will probably use these and other similar arguments to dissuade you from major political involvement. Somehow we in America have come to consider citizenship a passive thing — read the paper, gripe to friends, vote on election day, decry the results. Too many of us believe it is the duty of a good citizen to vote, but not to undertake to make the electoral process meaningful by actually participating.

The opposite ideal — everyone involved passionately, completely, and *only* in politics — is just as absurd. There are many aspects to life. The artist more dedicated to politics than art becomes a "social realist" or a reactionary demagogue, neither of which produces great art. The worker more concerned with politics than his vocation becomes essentially a patronage worker employed not for the daily job he does but for the work he does in the precincts at election time.

Nonetheless, unless some people at some time in their lives are willing to give most of their energies to politics and to working with political organizations in order to offer important alternatives to the voters, democracy is impossible. Some people must become active participants for more passive voters to have any meaningful role in shaping their government and society.

It can be important for everyone who would become a complete human being to participate actively at some stage in his life in the process of electing representatives and forming public policies. There is a strong relationship between weak ego strength, alienation, anomie, cynicism and non-participation, just as there is a relationship between participation and positive traits such as a sense of political efficacy and personal effectiveness.[2] People with a greater sense of efficacy and effectiveness and less alienation, anomie and cynicism are more likely to participate actively in politics which, in turn, reinforces their positive personal attitudes and undermines their negative attitudes. The Greeks, particularly, were very aware of the importance of political participation and recognized that the quality as well as quantity of activity is crucial to one's personal development. As Pericles said of Athens:

> Our citizens attend both to public and private duties, and do not allow absorption in their own various affairs to interfere with their knowledge of the city's. We differ from other states in regarding the man who holds aloof from public life not as 'quiet' but as useless . . ..[3]

There are other good reasons why it is especially important to be involved in politics at this particular time. We face in our country the necessity of renewing and reforming our entire political process from top to bottom, of reorienting our personal and societal priorities so as to place the value of people before property, concern for our fellow citizens at least on a par with concern for ourselves. If we lose this battle, our society will deteriorate into a closed society, into an eternal battleground of ever more violent factions, or into a fat, complacent, hedonistic culture. We have too much promise, too great a history to allow that to happen to us.

Few people join politics for such generalized reasons, however. They get into politics because there is a candidate they want to see elected or one that must, in their opinion, be defeated. There is an issue which they feel must be supported or opposed. Their friends are involved in a campaign or they find a particular movement, made up of particular people, which they wish to join. More than any other single factor, most people get into politics because *someone* they respect asks them to.

In addition to altruistic reasons for political involvement, there are more selfish reasons as well. Some people would like the status and honor of being an elected public official; some are desirous of being an administrative assistant to such officials; some have a more modest desire to be a leader within a community or political organization. Some people would simply like recognition for making a legitimate and important contribution to the political process.

All of us like to be recognized and honored for what we do. We desire the respect and the esteem of our fellows. In this sense all of us who go into politics have "political ambitions". There is nothing shabby or immoral about such ambitions — but politics has an amazing ability to corrupt. The general desire for honor and a position from which to best serve the community is a legitimate desire. The expectation of a particular "payoff" because of political involvement and, especially, the notion that there must be an immediate and tangible payoff is illegitimate. If you stay active in politics and help others to find meaningful participation in the political process, they will want to bestow honors upon you *but* not necessarily immediately and not necessarily the ones you expect.

The difficult part of politics is to become a legitimate political man or woman. To be political, one must have a sense for the use of power, but that alone is not enough. One must first and foremost be a person of honor, sensitivity, integrity, creativity, and responsive to other people's needs and concerns. To be an outstanding political leader, one must first be an outstanding person. Max Lerner has put the point this way:

> I don't hold it against a man that he has spent his mature life in politics, provided there is more to him than politics. The question about Richard Nixon is whether there is this "added dimension" (as he likes to call it) or whether the politician has eaten up the man.[4]

There are thus both altruistic and selfish reasons for political involvement. Self-interest in the broadest sense and honest concern for the community must be made to coincide. Only then can the kind of political people necessary to the creation of a new politics emerge.

Joining independent politics

There is one fundamental argument against going into independent politics. Many people, some of whom would seem to have the experience and the intelligence to know what they are talking about, will tell you that the only way to have a political effect on our society is by working through the existing political parties. They will tell you that these parties are over one hundred years old, that third parties never succeed, and that the existing parties are the political organizations which determine the make-up of our government at both the national and local levels. The only people who don't work within the parties, they will argue, are nonpolitical idealists or dogmatic revolutionaries.

The argument for working within the regular parties is not as strong as proponents would pretend; the record of those who would reform parties from within is not as good as it should be. Certainly their performance at national party conventions over the last decade is unimpressive. The liberals in the Republican party have been unable to keep the party from nominating men like Nixon, Agnew, Goldwater, and Miller. Liberal platform planks have consistently been defeated and the party is nearly completely closed to minority groups.

Nor have attempts to reform the Democratic party from within fared much better. The clash between party regulars and insurgents came to a head at the 1968 convention in which liberal platform planks on Vietnam were defeated, youths were clubbed outside the convention, and more popular candidates like McCarthy and McGovern were spurned in favor of Humphrey. Some rule changes were made at the convention, and the McGovern Commission has since developed a policy statement about more direct citizen participation — but these reforms have yet to be achieved.

Parties are difficult to reform — particularly those as fossilized and entrenched as the Republican and Democratic parties — so *competition,* not exhortation, is the best way to move them. If the parties know that whenever they nominate second-rate candidates they will have to run against independents with volunteer armies working for their election, as well as against opponents from the other party, they may learn the necessity for internal change. Should parties nominate good candidates and begin to take progressive stands on the new cleavages of our time, independents are free to join them and the independent movement will disappear.

If parties fail to reform, independent political organizations, not other parties, may well emerge as the potential framework for a new politics. In contrast to regular parties, independent organizations are dependent upon volunteers instead of patronage workers, issue-oriented instead of economically motivated, and composed of small, functional units rather than large, rigid hierarchies of power and authority. In effect, independents are saying to existing parties, "Send us the oppressed, the citizens fed up with the political process, the belligerent, the alienated, the ones for whom you can find no use; with their idealism and their labor we will create a more humane political system."

The reasons for backing an independent candidate or joining independent politics are ultimately as numerous as the people who do it. Listen to a sample of reasons why people backed Bernard Weisberg in his bid to be elected as delegate to the Illinois Constitutional Convention:[5]

> . . . because he is independent which is most important to me especially in a city like Chicago where the Democratic machine is so strong. (Student)

> . . . I think that there are people in this world that aren't getting a fair shake — Black people, poor people, young people and I'm trying to help remedy that situation. (Journalist)

> . . . Well I got sick and tired of having other people make the decision for me. I wanted to have a hand in making the decisions that affect my life, myself. So I became involved in independent politics. (Professor)

> . . . I think as a private citizen I have to do more than just gripe about bad government. I think we all have to work very hard to change it. I have added personal reasons in that I am a clergyman, and I feel if I really take seriously my concern for people and human problems and doing something about it, then I feel I have to do more than preach sermons on Sunday. And so I'm getting involved and what I'm most pleased about is that large numbers of my parishioners are beginning to take seriously what it means to be religious people, and to do something about their government by working for a good candidate such as Bernie Weisberg. (Catholic Priest)

The themes constantly repeated are a concern for people, dismay at the failures of the current political system, and a desire to be part of those crucial decisions that affect all our lives. If you agree with these sentiments, perhaps participatory politics is a valid way for you to express them.

Working in elections

Because participatory politics is so issue-oriented, many people want to dive immediately into issue battles. Paradoxically, the best way to deal successfully with the issues may be through electoral campaigns. It is easier to begin with a clear-cut and exciting election than to fight a separate issue battle. In an election it is known well in advance that the decisive event will be held on a certain date and that the result will be determined by a majority of the votes cast. The date for citizens to register, the rules of campaigning, and myriad procedural details are not only established but accepted. The public sees participation in elections as a familiar and proper activity.

Unfortunately, in an issue campaign it is hard to know who can make the decision you desire, much less the rules by which the decision is to be made. Often major business and political leaders with decision-making power are relatively isolated from the public; thus, it is difficult to pressure them directly. This is not to say that issue campaigns are impossible, simply that they are harder to fight and harder to win.

Moreover, if you are able to contest an election successfully, you may then be able to handle issues more easily. You will have built a strong organization and have the great advantage of being able to work with the official you have just elected. He can easily get publicity and introduce appropriate legislation which can provide a clear focus for the effort. So begin with elections, then turn your attention to the many issue battles which need fighting.

In the meantime encourage your candidate to address *some* of the critical issues while articulating his perspective on current problems. He can't take stands, especially extreme or novel stands, on *every* issue facing your community. If he does, he will make too many enemies, be counted an extremist and defeated at the polls. Instead, during the course of the campaign, a good candidate will dramatize only two or three concrete issues as examples of the kinds of steps he will take if elected. In a community where no issues have previously been debated or resolved, this is not a limitation, but a major beginning.

Among the many individual issues upon which a candidate is called to take a stand, some themes or issues are going to be more basic to the outcome of the campaign than others. Although campaign themes will be discussed in more detail in Chapter IV, they are important enough to be discussed briefly in this chapter as well. The biggest single problem (and opportunity) for a candidate is to define his own campaign in a way most likely to attract workers and voters.

In my own campaign for alderman, I developed a general appeal that transcended ethnic and interest groups by making it clear that I was an independent running against a Democratic Machine candidate. If I were elected I pledged that 1) citizens would receive their government services as a matter of right rather than as partisan favors, because I would open a full-time aldermanic office to serve all the people; 2) citizens would have a representative in City Council who would vote according to his conscience and constituents rather than simply rubber stamp the Mayor's legislation; and 3) citizens would have an opportunity to participate directly in government policy-making through the creation of a ward assembly with representatives from every precinct, representatives from every community organization, and monthly meetings open to the public, rather than a continuation of policy-making by a handful of party leaders. This stand in favor of a more participatory and fairer system of local government in machine-run Chicago placed the issue of the type of government we should have squarely before the electorate. Such stands, by themselves, were not enough to win, but they pointed up the importance of this election to both workers and voters. They are an example of the kinds of issues that ought, in my opinion, to be at stake in all elections.

A final warning. Some people will encourage you, because you are independent, to run an "educational campaign." By this slogan they mean that you should find a candidate who will take strong stands on issues — one who has never been involved in politics, at least with any winning campaigns — and back him even though you know that he will lose heavily. In theory, this candidate will make beautiful speeches and slowly begin the political education process in your district. The sad thing is that education campaign enthusiasts are right about the campaign being educational, but fail to understand what it teaches. *When a candidate gets only five or ten or twenty percent of the vote, the electorate concludes that it is stupid ever to back an independent candidate because it would just be throwing away votes.*

When politicians see such a result, far from being convinced to take a more courageous stand, it reconfirms their belief that they should not heed such radicals since they have no support in the community. *Never run a campaign with the intent of losing. Run to win, thereby educating the electorate to the fact that good men can be elected and teaching officeholders to mend their ways.* If you have a good candidate, organize well, and work hard, it should be possible to win. You won't win every election, but you must make a creditable try. A winning campaign, to a much greater extent than any "educational campaign," will convince more people to pay attention to issues, lead more people to join in the political process, and help bring about desired policy changes.

Initiating candidacies

There are two alternative strategies for an independent political organization in elections. Either it can endorse candidates after the parties have made their nominations or it can initiate candidacies. Whenever possible it is best for independents to sponsor their own candidates. First of all, when left to their own devices, parties rarely nominate outstanding candidates. Thus, a group which only endorses is left to choose between the Democrats' Twiddledee and the Republicans' Twiddledum. Not a very exciting beginning around which to build a campaign, much less a permanent organization. *It is much better to locate good candidates and let the parties make the choice whether or not to endorse your candidates.*

There is another important advantage to running your own candidate against those selected by the parties. A truly independent campaign builds permanent organizations more quickly and more soundly. Moreover, it immediately tests the strength of the independent movement in your district. When you back the candidate of one of the major parties, the independent voters and the party voters are inseparable — both can be claimed as the source of victory. When an independent candidate beats the candidates from both parties, the results are unambiguous and lay a firm foundation on which to proceed.

This is not to say than an independent organization or an independent citizen should never work for a regular party candidate. One should always work for the best candidate available in a particular election. Nor is it necessary that independents work for candidates running for every office, but simply for some of the best candidates at each election. Thus, all independent political organizations must at some time endorse candidates proposed by the parties. This frequently happens at general elections after all but two candidates running for office have been eliminated. Similarly, most independent organizations are too weak to successfully contest statewide or national races and must endorse party candidates at that level. There are, moreover, some positive aspects to endorsing party candidates. It provides an incentive for parties to offer better candidates and it permits the independent organization to compose a slate of good candidates for many positions in government, rather than sponsoring only a single candidate.

But when conditions make it possible to do so, independents should initiate their own candidacies and should not be afraid of opposing existing political parties. How to win such campaigns is what this book is really all about, although most suggestions apply to any volunteer, issue-oriented campaign.

A candidate's decision to run

A candidate decides to run for office for the same reasons you decide to get into politics — a combination of ambition and altruism. A good candidate decides much more readily to run if he has a chance to win, and a good candidate runs independently of the parties only if there are independent organizations to give him a base from which to launch the campaign. Briefly put, any candidate needs resources to win, if the potential for raising money, experienced staff, and workers in the time allotted to a campaign is not available from independents, a realistic candidate looks to the parties for support or decides not to enter the race at all.

A prime example of the importance of resources was the 1969

candidacy of Bill Singer for alderman on the north side of Chicago. A citizens' committee was formed to search for a candidate and Singer's name was one of many suggested. At the same time, the Independent Precinct Organization (IPO) needed to raise enough money to stay alive as an organization. Bill Singer and ten other men were called together at a luncheon and asked if they thought an aldermanic race was possible and then asked to write out checks to keep IPO alive until the election. They sat down and wrote out checks for a total of $800. When Bill Singer saw money raised so easily, he knew a tough campaign could be financed. When fifty representatives of community organizations showed up at citizens' committee meetings, he knew community support could be found. When IPO workers went door-to-door with petitions to get him on the ballot, he knew a campaign organization could be built. This kind of demonstration was necessary to get an able young lawyer like Bill Singer to run against the machine candidate in a district in which no independent had ever been elected. Good candidates want to know that the race, if they enter, will be a serious one and that they will get enough support to wage the kind of battle necessary to win.

Bernard Weisberg's statement about his candidacy further demonstrates that even though a man may hold a position of considerable prestige in his profession, even though many sacrifices may be required, it will be hard to say no if a group of citizens asks him to represent them:

> I never thought of running for office and I could easily see that becoming involved in the campaign would involve kind of a major disruption in my working life as a lawyer, my family life; and I wasn't sure that I really had an appetite for it. The more I thought about it the more negative I was, really. I could see it taking a tremendous amount of time, costing a pretty substantial amount of money and I was pretty much on the verge of saying definitely no until I suppose really two things began to weigh in my consideration. One was that I felt I really wouldn't feel very good saying no for the reasons that I

> mentioned already because it seemed to me that those weren't consistent with the idea of having some share in the responsibility that we all have really about government. And secondly, the more I thought about it, the more I was impressed with the suggestion . . . that running for office can be an educational experience which you really cannot get in any other way.[6]

Citizen decisions

Traditionally, a voter's decision as to whether he will vote and for whom has been influenced by his socio-economic position in society and by his identification with a political party.[7] Of less influence are a candidate's character, personality and stand on issues. Thus, one of the primary tasks of participatory politics is to reorient voters toward voting for the man and the issues, not the party and the pocketbook. Unless people like you get into politics, find qualified candidates to support, build strong campaign organizations capable of fielding an army of volunteers to talk with the voters, the parties will continue to make decisions out of narrow self-interest, based on meager information. Political reform begins with a single citizen's commitment. Political stagnation continues only because you and I fail to act.

Questions

This chapter has presented a number of basic issues which someone entering politics must confront. If you have understood the chapter, you should be able to answer the following questions. If you are uncertain as to your answers, feel free to refer back to pages in the handbook where the subject is discussed.

1. What reasons do you have for being involved in politics? Knowing your own motives, how might you expect to involve others?

2. Why would anyone choose to work with independent political organizations instead of within the parties? pp. 17-19.

3. What are the advantages in participatory politics of beginning with an electoral rather than an issue campaign? pp. 18-19.

4. What does an "education campaign" usually teach constituents? What does it usually teach opposing politicians? pp. 20-21.

5. What are two conditions which may convince good candidates to run for public office? What can you do to insure that these conditions are present? pp. 22-23.

6. What are frequently the two most crucial influences on how a citizen will vote? What factors would independents prefer to make dominant? p. 24.

Chapter III

Building a Volunteer Organization

Recruiting, funding, and organizing a virtual army of volunteers is the first priority of an independent campaign. It begins with the citizens' committee that selects the candidate, is augmented by a candidate's own resources, enhanced by the wise selection of leaders, shaped by the evolution of a functional structure, and completed by techniques of direct personal solicitation, political coffees and benefits. Every campaign activity must help to raise the hundreds of volunteers and the thousands of dollars necessary for success. If a volunteer army can be raised and equipped, election battles can be fought and won. If not, your political war is over before it is begun.

Each participatory campaign differs somewhat from all others, yet many principles and techniques remain the same. Since various Chicago campaigns over the last three years have developed certain aspects of campaigning to a greater extent than others, examples from these will be used to illustrate the techniques of participatory politics. But because campaigns are similar, a single campaign, that of Bernard Weisberg for delegate to the Illinois Constitutional Convention, will be used as a model throughout this handbook so that you can follow one campaign from start to finish.

The Weisberg campaign is a good example for several reasons. First of all, the documentary film *By The People* gives you a chance to actually see as well as read about the Weisberg campaign. Second, the race was run in a district with over seventy-five thousand registered voters and few local elections are run in larger districts. In fact, the same techniques could be used to elect mayors of medium-sized cities or congressmen in some states. Third, since it was not the first independent campaign we had run on the north side of Chicago, we had perfected most of the basic techniques by the time we undertook this campaign.

The 11th State Senatorial District

Since this handbook will often refer to the Weisberg campaign, perhaps a moment should be taken to describe the district in which that contest took place. The 11th district is located on the north side of Chicago, along Lake Michigan. It contains some 148 precincts split among three wards (44th, 46th and 48th.) The 76,306 voters of the district represent all economic classes — the wealthy living in high rises and mansions along the lake, professionals concentrated in a middle strip, and the working class and poor living primarily in the western section of the district.

FIG. 1
MAP OF 11th DISTRICT

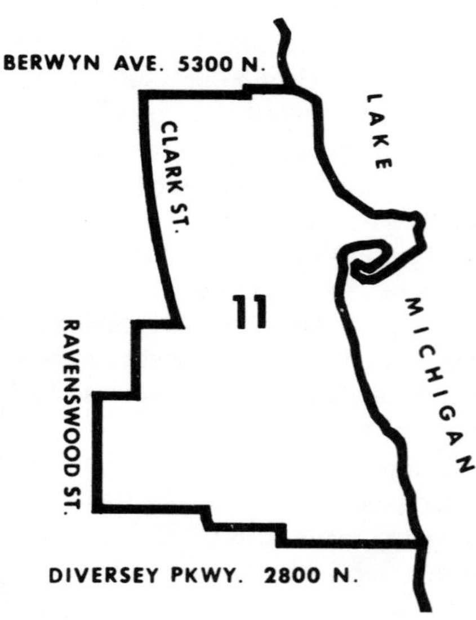

Politically, the regular Democratic party dominates the area. Traditionally the district has voted at least two-to-one in favor of Democrats. Although a few Republicans backed by independents have been elected, prior to 1969 independents had never won any victories on their own. In 1968 the attempt to elect McCarthy delegates to the Democratic National Convention failed in the wards of the district by a four-to-one margin.

Table 1

Election Results From The 1968 Primary, By Ward

Ward	Votes for Regular Delegates	Votes for McCarthy Delegates
44th	3,818	1,816
46th	4,347	1,185
48th	4,436	759
Total	12,601	3,760

The first success in the district was electing Bill Singer as an independent alderman from the 44th Ward in April, 1969. Bill won by a mere 427 votes in a close race which brought Singer (Independent Democrat) 12,091 votes and Gaughan (Regular Democrat) 11,664. In less than six months the four-to-one margin had been reversed and the historical pattern of electing only Democrats had been shattered. It was the first obvious victory in our attempt to alter Chicago politics. It was an election involving almost twenty thousand voters — more than vote in most towns and smaller cities throughout the nation. Yet this was only one ward. To win, Bernard Weisberg would have to do well in all three wards.

Selecting a candidate

The secret to success in candidate selection lies in a strong citizens' search committee which not only locates a worthy candidate, but lays the foundation for a broadly based coalition capable of mounting an effective campaign.

A citizens' committee should consist of leaders from all community, economic, ethnic, political, and religious groups which might support an independent candidate. Two to three months before candidate petitions must be filed, sixty to seventy people are invited by the leaders of the strongest community group or independent organization, and about fifty may actually appear. In constituting the committee, special care should be taken to ask all potential candidates or members of their families *not* to participate as committee members. Otherwise, the charge will be made that the committee was rigged from the beginning. Hopefully, community leaders, by meeting together, will discover that they have common interests and common problems, that a citizen-based campaign could be won, and that by electing an independent public official they could begin to work together to solve community problems.

The citizens' committee process is relatively simple, although two or three meetings are usually required for it to complete its task. Prior to the first meeting, the conveners make a list of twenty or thirty people who might be interested in being a candidate. The meeting is opened by a discussion of community problems, the up-coming election, ideal characteristics an office-holder should possess, and the feasibility of running a successful campaign. Additional candidates are added to the conveners' list and all potential candidates are discussed. Through discussion, the list is shortened to the five or six candidates the committee would like to interview.

Potential candidates are invited to the next meeting and questioned as to their willingness to run and what kind of campaign they would wage. After having made their presentations and departed, the potential candidates are discussed. The committee then either arrives at a consensus or agrees to take the names of several contenders back to their own groups for possible endorsement. A straw vote may be taken of the committee to indicate preferences, but the object is to reach a consensus that includes as many community leaders as possible. Since the leaders represent different groups and many are not even empowered to act on their group's behalf, a binding vote is not possible. Each group will follow its own endorsement procedures. Later, if there has been a consensus and if most groups have endorsed the same candidate, many of the people on the original committee will become members of the candidate's own citizens' committee and will work in his or her campaign.

A citizens' committee thus serves as a pre-test of a candidate's ability to mount an independent campaign in the community. For example, should the leaders of groups whose support would be crucial to success oppose the effort or the available candidates, then the campaign had best not be attempted. On the other hand, the committee locates potential candidates, narrows the field, and helps an acceptable candidate begin his or her campaign early enough to have a chance to win. Last of all, the citizens' committee is a mechanism for initiating a winning coalition by insuring that like-minded groups consider the same contenders in making endorsements. By the time the citizens' committee process is finished, a general consensus to back one or two candidates usually emerges, and this has the added benefit of deterring new independent candidates from entering the race and splintering the independent vote.

A candidate's resources

In selecting a candidate, it is important to be sure that he or she is a legitimate candidate in the eyes of the community. A young college student who has just recently moved into the community and who is likely to move away after graduation is an example of a candidate who is not credible. *Ideally, a person who has lived in the area for several years and who has visibly participated in previous community affairs is much to be preferred.*[8] In addition to identification with a particular community, a candidate also needs political credibility. A woman known for her cocktail parties and afternoon teas but who has never exhibited any leadership in political affairs may have difficulty in seeming a credible candidate.

Of course, a candidate must also meet all the legal requirements of residence, citizenship, and voter registration. It is important that this is researched carefully by the citizens' committee before it endorses any candidate. Nothing can be more destructive to the development of independent politics in a district than to undertake a major campaign only to have the candidate disqualified on a technicality.

More than simply being legal and credible, a candidate should not be a financial liability to the groups supporting him. He or she stands the most to gain from a victory in terms of personal prestige, power, and at least a modest salary; therefore, it is fair to expect them to willingly give some of their own money to the campaign. The candidate must usually donate or raise among family and friends the money necessary to open a headquarters, hire staff, and begin the campaign. In addition, he or she must be willing to raise funds — to ask people for money. No one can be timid in that respect and still expect funds to be raised by others. Moreover, a candidate should have enough supporters outside of the endorsing groups to supply some of the workers and campaign leaders. Although no candidate can supply all the money and workers needed to win a campaign, his or her personal contribution will set the tone for the sacrifices others will be willing to make.

There is one resource which must be absolutely demanded of a candidate, however, and that is time. He must canvass door-to-door in the toughest precincts, speak at public meetings, go to coffees, appear at campaign rallies, hold press conferences, appear on TV and radio as much as possible, give interviews to reporters, check over campaign plans, shake hands at bus stops and supermarkets, solicit organizational and newspaper endorsements, raise money, and greet guests at parties. Every day of candidacy is a full-time job, even if, for practical reasons, the candidate continues precampaign employment.

If you have been able to find a candidate who is credible, meets legal requirements, is intelligent, takes a stand on the important issues in the community, brings both some money and some workers to the campaign, commits himself twenty-four hours a day to the effort *and,* on top of all that, has a reasonably well-known name, you are extraordinarily lucky. Name identification by the average voter is difficult to achieve. Most advertising budgets in politics are spent just to get the voter to know that the candidate exists. So the better known your candidate is at the outset, the easier it will be to win the campaign — that is, if your candidate is not infamous.

Finally, if a candidate is articulate and his positions on critical issues are well developed, this will boost his candidacy. However, even if he or she does not possess these characteristics at the start, the months of constant speaking before groups inevitably improve a candidate and help him elaborate what had before been only the most tentative of opinions. As long as a candidate holds positions consonant with those of groups backing him, he or she can, with experience, become an effective spokesperson.

Don't be overly sensitive about shortcomings of your candidate's personality, especially since he or she will usually meet (for more than a handshake at the bus stop) only one or two thousand voters. A candidate is most important for recruiting workers and raising money. It is the workers who have the greater contact with individual voters. If your candidate is able to capture the support of potential workers, he will be able to learn during the campaign itself the necessary techniques to appeal to voters. A candidate who is too shy and retiring or too boisterous and self-centered will be transformed as the campaign gives him more exposure to people and as he gets feedback from campaign workers and staff. What is important is that your candidate be honest and responsive, genuinely concerned with people and their problems, and firm in his own beliefs. Finally, don't underestimate the voters. In my own campaign for alderman many workers assured me of their own support based on my positions on the issues and my past record. But they strongly urged me to smile more often for "the average voter." They feared that other voters would be less "perceptive" than they were. Two things happened. I learned to be more personable as the campaign progressed, while many voters voted for me for the same reasons campaign workers were willing to support me in the first place.

Selecting campaign leaders

In selecting campaign leaders one is faced with a number of basic decisions:

1. Should a candidate rely only on volunteers or pay salaries to part or all of the staff?
2. Should the key leadership be composed only of the candidate's personal friends, or should it include people from supporting organizations and new people discovered after beginning the campaign?
3. Should the key leadership be an exclusive group with the power to make decisions unilaterally, or should decisions be made in consultation with others in the campaign?
4. After the leaders are chosen, what authority do they have and what role does the candidate continue to have in campaign decision-making?

What specifically should be done regarding these decisions will differ according to the personalities and conditions of each campaign. However, a general description of the selection and role of the campaign staff may prove helpful.

To a great extent, the size of the district will determine the number of paid staff who will be necessary to run the campaign effectively. But in even the smallest districts a successful campaign will employ at least two or three of the following staff members: 1) campaign manager, 2) office manager, and 3) publicity chairman. Salaries are usually paid to these staffers because theirs are full-time campaign jobs which require from eight to fourteen hours a day. Since they must usually forego other employment to serve, it is normal to pay them at least minimal salaries unless they can afford to donate their time.

The key campaign officials, whether they are volunteers or paid staff, are usually selected on the basis of their skills and experience, their willingness to devote the time necessary to do the job well, and their loyalty to the candidate. No matter how experienced or skilled a campaign worker may be, he should not be made a part of the key leadership unless his dedication to the candidate and the campaign allows him to be trusted absolutely. If, after all these qualifications are met, it is possible to include in the inner circle members from the most important organizations backing the candidate, it is advantageous to do so. They will know how to utilize the organize their group's resources most effectively, and their presence in the campaign hierarchy will assure the organizations that their concerns are represented in the campaign decision-making process.

As Alderman Singer discovered in his campaign:

> The candidate must have confidence in the staff's ability to run the campaign, as he cannot run it himself. Likewise, the staff must have confidence in the candidate and his ability to see the issues and the problems of the campaign. The candidate is not going to be able to select all of the campaign personnel, and this should be particularly the job of the Campaign Manager who will select the persons responsible for running various aspects of the campaign. Of course, the Campaign Manager should consult the candidate on these selections. But the candidate should and must select a few key persons upon whom he is going to have to place great reliance, and this must be done early in the campaign. From that time on the most important thing for the candidate is exposure and personal contact. This can't be done from his office or on the telephone working out campaign problems.[9]

There are many campaign workers who play important roles in an independent campaign. Because of this and the nature of independent politics, a dilemma arises. Many decisions have to be made quickly and instructions have to be followed exactly by campaign workers if a campaign is to be successful. On the other hand, workers care about the campaign, have a right to participate in decisions that they are going to be called upon to effectuate, and can make perceptive contributions to campaign decision-making. A balance must be struck between the authority of campaign leaders and the right of workers to be a part of the decision-making process. Just as independents attempt to create a consultative and participatory democracy in society, so they must begin within the campaign itself to have consultation and participation. Key campaign leaders and staff members will undoubtedly meet in executive sessions several nights a week, but the total leadership should meet at least once a week. While immediate decisions will sometimes have to be made by key staff, individually or in executive session, long-range planning involving such areas as publicity, precinct work, and fund raising should be discussed in the larger weekly meetings and the advice of campaign workers heeded as often as possible.

Campaign structure

It is impossible to provide a definitive organization chart or job descriptions for campaigns because the structure varies according to the size of the campaign to be undertaken, the skills and experience of the leaders, the time each of the volunteers can devote, the number of workers available, and the personal relationships which exist or develop among members of the campaign. If we take the Weisberg campaign as an example, the campaign structure during the later stages might be diagrammed as shown on page (37). The leaders listed immediately beneath the candidate formed the executive committee although other campaign leaders also had major responsibilities. All leaders in the campaign had more or less explicit functions and were directly connected to the workers necessary to carry out these functions.

While there is a need for an explicit, hierarchical structure in order to complete the mammoth tasks of the campaign in time for the election, there is also a need for considerable communication and coordination both within and between structural units. The structure should allow for speedy communication within given functional areas so that the precinct coordinator is able to relay instructions to precinct workers and to receive precinct-by-precinct reports on the progress of the campaign. Such weekly or bi-weekly reports by precinct workers are critical in reminding workers of the tasks they have promised to perform, in allowing for effective campaign strategy and informed decision-making, and in providing for better control and the potential for corrective action.[10] Communication and coordination are needed between sections of the campaign as well. That is the reason for the

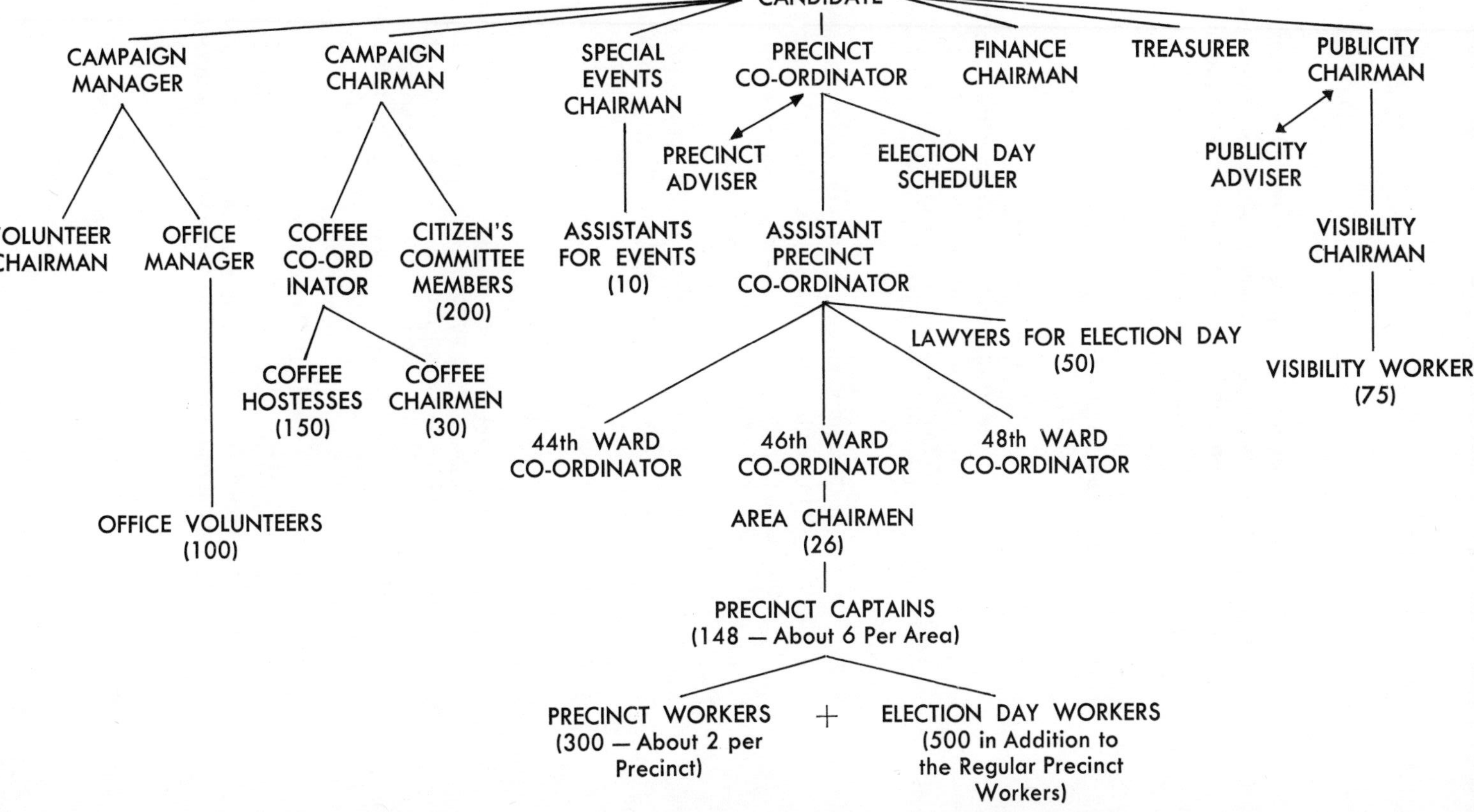
WEISBERG CAMPAIGN ORGANIZATION CHART
CANDIDATE
CAMPAIGN MANAGER
CAMPAIGN CHAIRMAN
SPECIAL EVENTS CHAIRMAN
PRECINCT CO-ORDINATOR
FINANCE CHAIRMAN
TREASURER
PUBLICITY CHAIRMAN
PRECINCT ADVISER
ELECTION DAY SCHEDULER
PUBLICITY ADVISER
VOLUNTEER CHAIRMAN
OFFICE MANAGER
COFFEE CO-ORD INATOR
CITIZEN'S COMMITTEE MEMBERS (200)
ASSISTANTS FOR EVENTS (10)
ASSISTANT PRECINCT CO-ORDINATOR
VISIBILITY CHAIRMAN
LAWYERS FOR ELECTION DAY (50)
VISIBILITY WORKERS (75)
COFFEE HOSTESSES (150)
COFFEE CHAIRMEN (30)
44th WARD CO-ORDINATOR
46th WARD CO-ORDINATOR
48th WARD CO-ORDINATOR
OFFICE VOLUNTEERS (100)
AREA CHAIRMEN (26)
PRECINCT CAPTAINS (148 — About 6 Per Area)
PRECINCT WORKERS (300 — About 2 per Precinct)
+
ELECTION DAY WORKERS (500 in Addition to the Regular Precinct Workers)

frequent executive sessions, the weekly leadership meetings, and the occasional sessions with all campaign workers—from the early months of the petition drive and registration campaign until election day. All of these structures, meetings, and reports are not meant to stifle but to promote creativity.

What jobs have to be done? What do the people whose names are entered on an organization chart agree to do?

Campaign Chairman

The chairman is head of the citizens' committee, chairman of weekly leadership meetings, and an important fund raiser. However, the job can be much more, as can any job in a campaign. Here is how Donald Page Moore described his tasks in *By The People:*

> The role of the campaign chairman isn't really definable. You've got to do a little bit of everything. You're in charge of hiring and firing people and finding people to do the multitude of tasks that have to be done. I've been involved in public relations, lawsuits, hiring a campaign manager, hiring an office manager, fund raising takes a lot of my time, recruiting lawyers to do poll watching on election day. I've done everything from sweeping out the headquarters to holding press conferences.[11]

Campaign Manager

A campaign manager coordinates the efforts of all other workers in the campaign, orders supplies, and makes the day-to-day decisions that keep a campaign moving. As Sherwin Kaplan of the Weisberg campaign used jokingly to say, a campaign manager works sixteen hours a day instead of the fourteen hours put in by volunteers.

Precinct Coordinator

The most essential role in any participatory campaign is that of precinct coordinator. It is this man or woman who puts the precinct organization together, conducts training sessions, constantly receives workers' reports, and coordinates collection of petition signatures, voter registration drive, voter canvasses, and election day activities.

Finance Chairman

The job of finance chairman, treasurer, and purchase officer are sometimes combined and sometimes separated. The tasks are 1) raising the money, 2) determining what expenses can be afforded, and 3) locating the cheapest suppliers of buttons, flyers, printing, posters, and any other commodities necessary to the campaign.

Publicity Chairman

The publicity or public relations chairman coordinates the production of all publicity, including brochures, buttons, bumper stickers, posters, news stories, TV and radio programs. June Rosner, the Weisberg publicity chairman, summarized her job thus: "Basicially my job is to get the candidate's name familiar with the voters and build the sort of image for him that will make workers enthusiastic to work in the campaign."[12]

Office Manager

The office manager is responsible for work done in the campaign headquarters. The latter includes keeping records of all potential workers, mailings, mimeographing campaign literature, typing letters, preparing for rallies and training sessions, telephone campaigns, and simply answering the ever-ringing campaign telephones.

Coffee Coordinator

A good coffee coordinator or team of coordinators will, by the end of the campaign, have convinced over one hundred families to host a coffee, delivered to these hosts the appropriate campaign materials including instruction sheets and invitations, recruited and trained dozens of coffee chairmen, scheduled and briefed the candidate for each appearance. These hundred or more campaign coffees are critical to recruiting volunteers, raising money, and meeting voters.

Visibility Chairman

Because name identification is so important, a visibility crew, often made up of high school and college students, is created to insure that hundreds of posters are placed in windows of homes and stores; that lampposts throughout the district are covered (preferably with posters attached with wire so that they can be removed when the campaign is over), and that as many people as possible be induced to wear campaign buttons. This hard-working crew is coordinated by the visibility chairman.

Area Chairmen

The critical middle management of participatory campaigns are the area chairmen. Each area chairman coordinates from four to six precincts. They recruit many of the precinct workers; provide the workers with materials, instructions, and assistance with problems in the precinct; collect reports from all precincts under their supervision. Thus, area chairmen are the key communications link in the campaign. Their reports and suggestions at the weekly leadership meetings are essential to decisions to alter the direction of the campaign, to intensify the effort, or simply to proceed with current plans because the campaign is having the desired effect on the voters.

Recruiting workers

In West Africa there is a saying, "Nothing can be done without money." Whether a road needs to be built, a marriage contracted, or a man elected chief, the answer is always the same. In participatory politics a more appropriate saying would be: "Nothing can be done without workers." No workers, no campaign.

Since volunteers are so necessary to a successful campaign, recruiting them is a major concern underlying every action, although three methods are most frequently used. The first, which is used so often and so naturally that it often goes unnoticed, is direct contact. Campaign workers tell their friends and acquaintances about the campaign and sign them up as volunteers. This same form of direct, person-to-person recruiting is used more systematically by the campaign leadership. When a person is appointed area chairman and must recruit twenty precinct workers to canvass the precincts he supervises or a coffee coordinator must find a hundred coffee hostesses, they begin with a list of prospective workers. These lists are garnered from supporting organizations, from prior political campaign files, from lists of friends and acquaintances, and from lists of people who have already volunteered to help in this campaign but have yet to be given a specific task. The campaign official then goes to the telephone and personally calls each prospect and asks them to volunteer for specific tasks. If the original lists are insufficient, then he will have to go door-to-door or phone all registered voters in an area until enough volunteers can be found to get the job done.

In addition to direct contact, coffees and social events make an ideal occasion for citizens to meet the candidate, to evaluate him, and to be converted into volunteers. A "coffee" is a campaign meeting in a volunteer's home to which the neighbors are invited to hear the candidate speak, and the name derives from the fact that coffee and cookies are frequently served as refreshments. Coffees have been used so often and so effectively in independent politics in Chicago that a more or less explicit formula for success has been developed. It begins with the hostess or several hostesses inviting their friends *and* every registered voter in one or more precincts. Although mimeographed invitations such as the one shown on page 44 are mailed to friends and placed in the mail boxes of voters, it is essential that the hostess personally phone and invite as many potential guests as possible. Of those who receive only the mimeographed invitation, one or two out of a hundred will appear, but as many as twenty-five to thirty percent of those called personally often come. Therefore, the telephone calls are essential to a good coffee.

To quote Bob Houston, an expert coffee chairman who drafted the coffee chairman's instructions for the Bruce Dumont campaign which are on page 42, "No coffee is ever a failure."[13] If only the hostess and one other person show up, at least the neighbors have been invited and know that the candidate has been in their own neighborhood to meet with his constituents. Moreover, the hostess and the other person attending the coffee can both be signed up to do precinct work which can affect hundreds of voters. Regardless of how many people attend a coffee, it is important that the maximum result be achieved. Coffee results are measured precisely by the number of volunteers and the contributions collected at the end of the evening.

WHAT EVERY *GREAT* COFFEE CHAIRMAN HAS TO KNOW

1. Get to the meeting *promptly,* preferably 15 minutes before the announced time.

2. Introduce yourself and, while awaiting the gathering of the group, remind the hostess to have all her guests sign the attendance sheet as they come in. Pass out DuMont literature to the guests as they arrive.

3. Call the meeting to order in time for introductory remarks before Bruce arrives. (This should usually be done about 20 minutes after the announced time of the coffee.) These are the principal points to cover:

   a. Briefly (2 minutes) discuss Bruce DuMont's background and the importance of having a full-time, independent-minded senator for our district. Check that everyone has received Bruce's biography.

   b. Review the facts of the election:
   - The election is Tuesday, November 3rd.
   - Bruce DuMont is running for state senator (emphasize state senator, or some voters will be confused and wonder whether he is running against Adlai Stevenson for U.S. Senate.)
   - We will elect one state senator from our district and our choice is between Bruce DuMont who is running on the Republican ticket and the incumbent Robert Cherry who is running on the Democratic ticket.
   - No one else is running for state senator.
   - We can split our ballot. (Stop and ask if there is any question on that.)
   - Any voter who registers by September 25 at City Hall or in the precinct Tuesday, October 5, may vote in this election.
   - We do not declare our party affiliation at this election.

   c. Go around the circle asking the guests what particular issues concern them most or what questions they would like Bruce DuMont to cover. (make notes)

4. When Bruce arrives (45 minutes after the time for which the meeting was set), stop. The hostess should introduce him to the group, individually. Briefly tell Bruce what issues are uppermost in the group's mind. After he speaks, he will answer questions until it is time for his next meeting. Generally, he should not stay more than 30 minutes.

5. *You, not DuMont, are the climax of the evening.* When, after answering all questions, Bruce leaves, take over. Do not let the group drift apart. Make a pitch for *workers, money,* and more *coffees* to wage a successful campaign.

   How do you make a successful pitch? One way is to say that you are not here to persuade anyone to do anything for Bruce, but to explain what they can do if they want him elected. Then explain what each item on the pledge card means. Conclude by urging each person to make up his mind, *now,* what, if anything, he wishes to do, to fill out his card *now,* and to give it to you *now.* Mention checks should be made payable to Citizens for DuMont. Then be silent. Discourage further conversation and answer any questions briefly. You want a little "embarassed silence" to make people settle down to committing themselves. Thank each person enthusiastically as they give you a card. Smile at them understandingly if they don't give you a card (they're still voters), but judge your success by how many workers you get signed up and how much money you receive.

6. It is important that you turn the pledge cards, money, chairman's report, and attendance sheet into headquarters at the end of the evening, so that we can follow up on our potential workers the next day. If headquarters is closed by the time you get there, put everything, including the leftover literature, in the mailbox.

7. Thanks and congratulations. If you have any questions, call headquarters, or Jeanne Sullivan.

Please be our guest to meet:

BERNARD WEISBERG

Candidate
for Delegate to the Illinois Constitutional Convention.
An independent—endorsed by the Better Government Association, the city's major newspapers and the Independent Voters of Illinois.

He will be at: Eadie Baron & Marion De John ~~1327 W. George St. - 2nd Floor~~

at: 7:00 PM, ~~Friday, October 31st~~ 1969

SPECIAL GUEST: Alderman Bill Singer
FESTIVE REFRESHMENTS!

Plese come and bring your friends.

How do you maximize the results? A chairman is assigned to cover the coffee. As the guests arrive, he and the hostess have them sign an attendance sheet, introduce them to the others in the group, and hand them campaign literature to read. Usually about twenty minutes after the announced time of the coffee, the chairman will call the meeting to order, discuss very briefly the background of the candidate and review facts about the election such as the date of election, how many candidates citizens may vote for, who the candidates are and how citizens may register to vote. Then, the guests are asked what particular issues concern them or which ones they would most like the candidate to discuss.

The candidate arrives about forty-five minutes after the time for which the meeting was set, and the hostess introduces him to each guest. Usually, the candidate will shake hands as he is introduced. The chairman will tell the candidate the questions about which the group has expressed the most interest and the candidate will speak and answer questions for about half an hour. In a very complicated campaign like the election of delegates to rewrite the state constitution Bernard Weisberg sometimes spent slightly more time at critical coffees, but it is terribly important that candidates be brief and not stay until all the fire has gone out of the meeting.

A candidate can make from three to five coffees a night if he keeps his remarks brief and to the point. That means you can multiply exposure of your candidate by carefully timing the coffees. In larger districts coffees can even be organized around a TV appearance by the candidate; thus his exposure can again be greatly maximized.

The chairman, not the candidate, is the climax of a successful coffee. The pitch is crucial. You need to explain why help is needed, what needs to be done, and to urge people *to make up their minds by filling out a pledge card and giving it to you before they leave.* The pledge card used in the Weisberg campaign is shown on page 46. It allows voters to indicate which ways they will contribute to the campaign. Be sure to thank each person who commits himself and to judge your own success by how many workers sign their cards and how much money you raise. The pitch can be very straight and hard — although the people in the room are voters, they don't have to like you. That's one of the reasons you make the pitch rather than the candidate. An example of such a pitch is the one given by Donald Page Moore at a Weisberg coffee:

> The machine is tough and we beat one machine candidate by 1600 votes and the other beat us by 115 votes [in the primary] . . . . So if we're going to win, we can only do it in a couple of well-recognized ways. One, we've got to have money and we can't shake the money out of people the way the county assessor's office does. It's going to cost us $35,000 to run a decent campaign for Bernard Weisberg. And this leaves us with about $20,000 to raise in the next six weeks. I don't see any point in making a secret about it, those are the facts. We've got fifteen in and we've got twenty to go. And if we don't get the money, we can't

win the election because we can't run an effective campaign without money . . . . Precinct work and election day work are fundamental. They're vital. They can be fun. You can be part of something that really means something for the future of this town. And we can't do it without it. We can't get by with 850 workers on November 18th. If we've only 850 workers on the street we're going to get buried . . . .

Citizens for ⊗ **BernardWeisberg**

Yes, I will help to elect Bernard Weisberg as delegate to the Illinois Constitutional Convention.

Name__________________________________Phone______________

Address______________________________Bus. Phone______________

I will:

- ☐ Join the Citizens Committee
- ☐ Do precinct work
- ☐ Give a coffee party
- ☐ Work in the headquarters
- ☐ Work on the election day
- ☐ Contribute $__________

719 W. Sheridan Road, Chicago, Illinois 60613 Phone 929-0755

And don't listen to this talk that Weisberg's got it in the bag. All that means is we're running up front. We've got a whale of a chance and they can beat the daylights out of us if we don't keep up the momentum. Now we can do it, but it is not in the bag and we need help desperately.

We need 1500 workers on the street election day, working

in the polling places, passing out literature, helping run the pluses [voters favorable to your candidate], helping make the phone calls — everything that has to be done on election day.

We need at least 1,000 precinct canvassers working in between now [and then] — in their, you know, the odds and ends of their week: on the weekends a few hours, in the evening a few hours. We've got to have it. If we don't have it, we get beat. And all these months and months of work and dedication and hope and all the rest of it go right down the drain. A dying machine is going to get a terrific shot in the arm and independent politics on the northside lakefront of Chicago is going to get a kick in the tail that will set it back for five years . . . .

It's terribly, terribly important. People all over this city . . . people in city hall, people in political headquarters all over this city are watching this and one or two other races in the city of Chicago to see what happens. To see if the independents can make it stick or are they going to run out of gas after a couple of cheap wins. That's what they are asking themselves and the political future of this state to some extent [depends on the outcome] . . . .

Let me just put it to you, *will you help?* Will you take some personal responsibility to help us here? I've got some cards that I'd like to pass out. They've got blanks for your names and addresses, squares you can check off if you are willing to work in a precinct, if you are willing to work election day, if you are willing to work in our headquarters between now and election day. This is in your spare time. It can be a tremendous experience.

Please join with us. If you can't give time, give money. If you can't give money, give time. If you can, do both. If you can't do either, vote for us.[14]

The third means of getting volunteers is to make use of every campaign event as a recruiting device. Start with the citizens' committee that selected the candidate in the first place. Each member should be called and asked to serve in some capacity with the campaign — at the very least, to lend their name to the campaign citizens' committee and their money to the campaign effort. Not only should people be recruited to work in the petition drive, every person who signs a petition to get your candidate on the ballot should receive a personally signed thank you letter from the candidate along with a pledge card and a request to join the campaign. Every time precinct workers go door-to-door they should not only seek to register people or get their vote, they should constantly be looking for potential workers to help with the campaign. Every person who comes into the headquarters to see what the campaign is all about should be put to work and later convinced to help out in the precincts as well. When the candidate shakes hands at bus stops or supermarkets, he should take pledge cards with him and sign up new workers on the spot. Every campaign effort, from stories in the newspapers to rallies in the park, should have pay-offs in terms of recruiting new workers for the volunteer campaign army as well as in affecting as many individual voters as possible.

Raising money

It should be obvious from the discussion about recruiting workers that money is raised in the same way — through personal contact, intimate social gatherings, and campaign events. But before much money can be raised you have to know how much is needed. To know that, you have to know something about campaign expenses and budgets.

As the three budgets in Table 2 illustrate, a successful independent campaign such as the Weisberg campaign may cost $.50 per voter in the district or more. Other campaigns which spend less may lose and certainly efforts like the personal campaign of an individual running alone are unlikely to succeed. Few successful campaigns will be run in districts of any size for less than fifteen to twenty thousand dollars. Of the money raised, salaries and publicity costs alone will use up over sixty percent of the budget. Add to this normal headquarters expenses, and most of the budget is spent. Your first thousand votes are cheap — almost free because you will get three to five percent of the vote just by getting your candidate's name on the ballot, and a hard-working candidate by himself can gather from five hundred to a thousand more votes. But the voters get progressively harder to reach. The next few thousand votes require a headquarters and staff and publicity. Ultimately, when you get within a few thousand votes of victory, you begin paying for advertising, extras like bumper stickers and car tops, and all that costs more and more money.

Once you have established a realistic budget for your campaign, you can set out to raise the necessary funds. Hank Parkinson in his book *Winning Your Campaign* quotes Iowa's Thomas Murphy as advising: "The best way to get money is to ask for it — the more people you ask, the more money you're going to get."[15] Or as Donald Page Moore of the Weisberg campaign put it, "It you're not afraid of losing friends, go to everybody you know — tackle them in the hall, phone them, write them a letter and then call them and simply say 'Give me money.' They will because it is right."[16]

In the Weisberg campaign only ten percent of the funds came from large contributions of $100 or more. Another twenty-five percent of the budget was raised through benefits. The remaining sixty-five percent came through innumerable small contributions. The large contributions were obtained primarily through individual contact and an important party at which former Senator Wayne Morse spoke. The benefits, which raised twenty-five percent of the budget, stressed imagination — something different than the usual politician's dinner. The biggest benefit, given after the campaign, was held at one of the architectural landmarks in the district and featured a harp and piano concert in which the candidate himself played the piano.

Based on our experiences in Chicago, planning for a successful benefit should consider carefully the following rules of thumb:

Table 2

Budgets For Three Types of Independent Campaigns For Delegate to the Constitutional Convention in Illinois, 1969

	Weisberg Campaign			Strong Independent Contender			Individual Running Without Support	
Item	*Cost*	*% of Budget*		*Cost*	*% of Budget*		*Cost*	*% of Budget*
1. Printing, Public Relations, Advertising	$13.300	39	(Printing alone — 36%	$ 6.850	27		$ 300	100
2. Salaries	7.300	22		9.900	40		0	0
3. Rent, Office Equipment & Supplies	3.800	11		2.650	11		0	0
4. Postage	3.800	11	28% Head-quarters Expenses (items 3–5)	1.850	7	27% (items 3–5)	(Counted in P.R.)	
5. Telephone	2.200	6		2.400	9		0	0
6. Miscellaneous Petty Cash Expenditures	3.000	9		100	1		0	0
7. Parties (refreshment)	290	1		600	2		0	0
8. Political Contributions	250	1		600	2		0	0
TOTAL CAMPAIGN COST	$35.000	100%		$25.000	99%		$ 300	100%
Deficit still to be raised after campaign was over	$10.000	29%		$10.000	40%		$ 0	0%
Final Vote	Weisberg 15.301 Leading Democrat 13.171			Independent 7.949 Leading Democrat 14.770			Independent 2.328 Leading Democrat 19.383	
Money Spent Per Vote Received	$2.35			$3.10			$0.13	
Cost Per Voter in District	$0.46			$0.36			½¢	

1) It should be different from any previous benefit.

2) It should only be attempted if there are at least six weeks in which to make preparations and sell tickets.

3) The main event or entertainment must be donated. When you pay actors or performers, the event soon costs so much that you make no profit. With donated talent, you can make close to one hundred percent profit.

4) The rental of facilities should be relatively inexpensive.

5) Special invitations, flyers, and tickets should be printed for the benefit, if possible, to make it seem special and worth the price.

6) The price per person must either be relatively high ($50 or more) or relatively low ($5 or so). With the higher price, you shoot for an audience of at least a hundred. With the lower price you shoot for an audience of a thousand. If you use the lower price, more money can be raised by using special sponsor tickets at $25 or $50 and by selling advertisements in a program.

Nearly every campaign will have one or more benefits to raise money. If you keep them few in number, really concentrate on making those successful, leave plenty of time for preparations, and keep the overhead costs as low as possible, you can raise enough money to make the effort worthwhile.

Most money in independent campaigns is raised from small contributions of less than one hundred dollars. There are several reasons why this is desirable as well as necessary. First of all, every person in the district who contributes even a dollar is likely to vote for your candidate and actively encourage other citizens to do so. Secondly, many contributors will also be convinced to become coffee hosts or chairmen, office volunteers, or precinct workers. Third, every contributor feels that they own a piece of the campaign and, in fact, they do. A broad base of contributors means that constituents rather than a few rich men control their own representative. Thus, sufficient money cannot and should not be raised from only a few contributors. Independents seek the support of the innumerable small contributors because their financial assistance is the only source of money which will allow them to win without selling out to limited and special interests.

How are small contributions solicited? An original letter and pledge card sent to potential supporters of the candidate brings some money, as does the thank you letter and plea for help sent to petition signers. (The Simpson letter to petition signers is shown on page 53.) Some money comes unsolicited through publicity. A large amount of money is raised from among the campaign leaders and workers. But like recruiting volunteers, most small contributors are convinced to contribute by individualized contact with the candidate at coffees and social events at which the potential contributor knows that *he* or *she* is really important because so much time and attention is lavished on them. And the contributor is given a chance to make an extensive evaluation of the candidate first hand. The level of contribution coming from such an individualized contact is inevitably greater than the more impersonal letters.

Even with the large number of small contributions the job of raising larger contributions must also be undertaken. In my own campaign for alderman we worked hard to increase the number of $50 and $100 contributions through a series of luncheons. Many people who were far from wealthy were convinced through these sessions to make a larger contribution than they had generally given to political campaigns in the past, and previous donors were able to join the host and I for lunch at some convenient restaurant. Over drinks and during the lunch I discussed the campaign and what it meant to Chicago political reform, and the host or luncheon chairman told of our plan to get one hundred $100- and one hundred $50-sponsors. He then asked the people present to become a sponsor. At no luncheon did we raise less than $250, and through the series of luncheons we raised

Citizens for Simpson.

CAMPAIGN CHAIRMAN
nard Weisberg
NORARY CHAIRMEN
Alderman Bill Singer
Representative Bruce Douglas

HEADQUARTERS
1045 West Belmont
Chicago, Illinois 60657
Phone 525-6034

December 21, 1970

Dear Citizen,

Today I filed nominating petitions signed by you and 3500 neighbors. Because of your trust and assistance I will be able to mount a strong campaign for 44th ward Alderman. I hope in this campaign to address myself to the rights of citizens - to services, to a voice in local government and to responsible representation. I also plan to discuss such ward problems as schools, housing and traffic congestion. I hope to hear your views on all these issues during the course of the campaign.

Some of you I have known for years. Many more, I have met briefly on street corners and coffees during the last few weeks. But many of you have met only my campaign workers. However, well we may know each other, I would be pleased to have you attend the official opening of our headquarters at 1045 W. Belmont from 4 - 6 p.m. on Sunday, January 3rd. Speeches will be brief, refreshments modest and entertainment plentiful. It will be an opportunity not only to meet me but also to meet, and perhaps to join, all the great people working in this campaign.

Ours is a citizens campaign. You have made possible a beginning. If we are to continue and to win the election February 23rd, we need your help. If you can not make the headquarters opening please fill out the bottom of this page, cut out, and mail to main office.

Once again, thank you for signing my petitions. I hope to wage an honest, forceful campaign and, if elected, to conduct myself in office so as to be worthy of your trust.

Yours faithfully,

Dick Simpson

Dick Simpson
Candidate for Alderman
44th Ward

- -

Yes I want DICK SIMPSON for my alderman. I will:

Work in a precinct. Work in headquarters.
Host a coffee discussion with the candidate.
I know it costs money to campaign. Here's $__________.
Please add my name to Citizens' for Simpson Committee.
I can make a special contribution by ______________.
I will display a poster.

NAME______________ ADDRESS________________ ZIP________

HOME PHONE____________________ WORK PHONE________________

more than $3500. Without them, our campaign debt would have been that much greater.

Many people are understandably timid or reticent about requesting contributions from their friends, much less from strangers. While I have found it easy to raise money for others, I found it difficult to ask it for myself. But I have learned that a certain frame of mind is required for successful fund raising. You have to know that the contribution is really important no matter how large or small. You need to think of yourself not as someone begging on the street corner but as offering others the opportunity to give to something worthwhile, something that matters. When you give others the chance to give themselves to a good cause, a cause to which you have already pledged your time and money, you are not begging for crumbs but offering them the opportunity to make the same kind of commitment.

When people contribute money to the campaign, they must receive immediately (within the week) a personally signed thank you letter from the candidate. For all but very large contributors a neatly printed letter on campaign stationery (such as the one on page 55) is sufficient if the person's name is individually typed in the salutation. But this letter needs to be carefully composed and it must be signed by the candidate himself. People you thank early in a campaign can be called upon to contribute again if you are in desperate straits at later stages. Fail to thank them and they will not contribute to your campaign again and they may not contribute to future participatory campaigns.

Questions

1. How does a citizens' committee proceed in order to carry out its primary functions? pp. 30-31.

2. Of all beneficial traits and resources a candidate may bring to a campaign, what things must be demanded of him? If a candidate cannot be expected to meet every voter personally, what is his chief task? pp. 32-33.

3. To what extent can a campaign rely solely on volunteer leaders?

Citizens for Simpson.

CAMPAIGN CHAIRMAN
Bernard Weisberg
HONORARY CHAIRMEN
Alderman Bill Singer
Representative Bruce Douglas

HEADQUARTERS
1045 West Belmont
Chicago, Illinois 60657
Phone 525-6034

December 13, 1970

Dr. & Mrs. Edwin Levine
424 West Melrose Street
Chicago, Illinois 60657

Dear Hedda & Ed,

I am very grateful for your gift to my campaign for Alderman of the new 44th Ward.

Your willingness to contribute materially to politics is so important at this time, when many despair of achieving constructive political change and others refuse to recognize the need for change.

Knowing that we must make our political institutions responsive to the public and assuming responsibility for making them responsive -- these are the marks of the new political man. This is really what our campaign is all about; this is what your gift supports.

Again, my thanks to you. I will put forth my best effort to deserve your confidence.

Yours faithfully,

Dick Simpson

Dick Simpson

DS:bu

1045 West Belmont Avenue
Chicago, Illinois 60657 PHONE: 525-6034

Why do any of the staff need to be paid? p. 34.

4. What are some primary characteristics to be considered in selecting key campaign officials? Who usually selects them? pp. 34-35.

5. Why do workers need to be consulted at all in campaign decisions? On what kind of decisions are they most profitably consulted? p. 35.

6. Why is reporting so crucial in a campaign? How does the hierarchical structure facilitate this? How is coordination and cooperation between functional units facilitated? pp. 36-37.

7. What are the primary methods used in recruiting volunteers? pp. 40-41, 48.

8. Why is the chairman rather than the candidate the climax of a successful coffee? How is the success of a coffee measured? Why is no coffee ever a failure? pp. 41-45.

9. What is the best way to get money for a campaign? p. 48.

10. What percentage of funds should you expect to raise from large contributors, benefits and small contributors, respectively? What can you expect to be the major expenses of the campaign? pp. 49-52.

Chapter IV
Getting Known

Although public relations is normally used simply to get brand name recognition, in independent politics its purpose is not only to get voters to know the candidate's name and the office for which he is running, but also to attract workers and money to the campaign. The image and theme of the campaign must be powerful enough to achieve these ends and must be specifically developed by means of various communication tools such as press conferences, news releases, and campaign literature. All of this must take place within the time limits set by a realistic campaign schedule and be governed by a knowledge of the media to be used.

In participatory politics public relations serves three basic functions: 1) to get voters to recognize the candidate's name and to have a generally positive perception of him, 2) to attract the workers and financial contributions necessary to reach the voters through a door-to-door canvass, and 3) to express positive images and programs of political improvement which really distinguish independent from regular party candidates. To accomplish the practical purposes of raising resources, informing voters, and setting forth programs of change, public relations chairmen create an image for the candidate and the campaign. As Don Rose, the publicity adviser in the Weisberg campaign, explained the process:

> The important thing is to establish early an identity for the candidate, a point of reference for the candidate, assuming, as with most independents, that this is a guy without a broad public image or a well-known personality to begin with.[17]

It is crucial in building a candidate's image to begin with the real man and not some ideal type. A homebody can't be made into a swinger or vice versa. Bernard Weisberg was a concerned, liberal lawyer who had been long identified with the American Civil Liberties Union. Therefore, his public relations chairman naturally stressed his capability as a lawyer and his concern for the Bill of Rights in the new constitution. Because he was running an independent campaign, the image of an honest citizen battling the corrupt Chicago machine was also used. Don Rose described the image this way:

> The other reality, that is, the image of a man of the people, as it were — ordinary citizen fighting against the political machine [was stressed]. It's one that is necessary . . . You do have a constituency of active people who are going to join such a fight, and you have to make clear that this is going to be one of those fights not only for all the good things in life and for constitutional reform, but a major battle, a chance to diminish or neutralize the machine that has been oppressing this city for so long.[18]

One key to success in independent politics is the ability to dramatize and distinguish a campaign from all the other races occurring all over the state — to signal to the media, the voters, and potential workers that your campaign is one of the major political battles worth fighting. In the Weisberg campaign, distinguishing it from other races was made easier because Weisberg filed a lawsuit charging that the Secretary of State listed friends and party regulars at the top of the ballot, a position guaranteed to give them several hundred additional votes. With the mass media, action is the best way to attract attention and coverage. Thus, before the campaign had barely begun, Weisberg was jousting with one of the most powerful political bosses in the state. Winning his case brought not only good publicity for months to come, but it opened up the electoral process for other candidates and Weisberg himself was moved up from fifth place to second in the drawing for ballot position. This kind of demonstrative action reinforces and augments the image of a candidate and his campaign.

The uses of a campaign theme

A campaign theme unifies the campaign, defines the battleground on which you wish to fight, and conveys as briefly as possible information about the talents or character of the candidate and the issues at stake in the election. The theme may be simplified into a slogan or it may remain implicit in the campaign literature. For example, in the campaign to elect John Stevens alderman of the 42nd ward in 1969, all literature stressed the simple theme: *Stevens For Change.* In a district with predominantly white, conservative representatives of the Democratic party machine, the slogan reflected the fact that an independent black candidate was running, one desirous of healing the racial breach in the ward and of eliminating machine domination.

Another example of explicit campaign themes was the wording of a poster in the McCarthy campaign for President in 1968. It carried the simple inscription: *He Stood Up Alone and Something Happened.* The lone figure of McCarthy and this slogan captured both McCarthy's courage in putting his political career on the line to challenge an incumbent president of his own party and the chain of successful, grass-roots primary battles that had followed.

The choice of a theme is particularly important *in defining the issues in a way that a majority of citizens can identify with your candidate.* Thus you present your candidate to the voters as a qualified, "good government" candidate rather than as an idealistic radical. While you choose to make you fight about important issues, it is also critical that you try to cut the issues and define the alternatives in a way that the majority of citizens can support your candidate. Thus, you will want to distinguish your candidate from his opponents in strongly positive terms: an honest man vs. crooked politicians; an independent vs. the political machine; peacemaker vs. warmaker; competence vs. incompetence; a representative of the people vs. a representative of special interests.

While the stress is primarily placed upon your candidate's positive characteristics rather than on the opponent's faults, the contrast between them is important. These themes and images do not have to be made explicit and sloganized in every case. For example, buttons and

He stood up alone and something happened!

McCARTHY

OUR CHOICE '68!

M

STUDENTS
FOR
McCARTHY

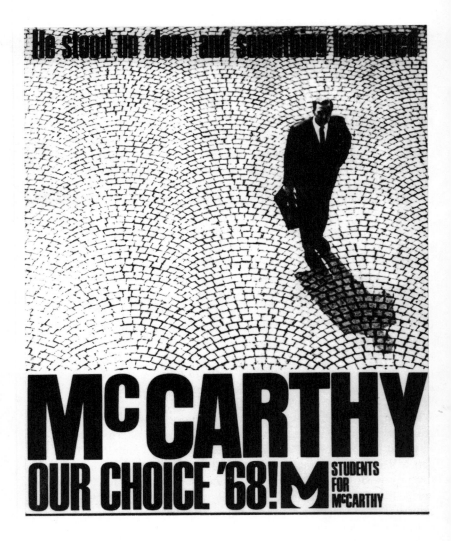

⊗Weisberg
Yes!

posters are used primarily for name identification and encouragement of the workers, and may often bear only the candidate's name and the office he is seeking. Even in more detailed campaign literature, slogans may not be necessary to make your point. For instance, in the Weisberg campaign, despite the fact that slogans were not used, it was clear on all campaign literature that Weisberg 1) was running against the Chicago machine, 2) was running to help to create a fairer, more equitable system of government in Illinois, 3) was a man of considerable legal talent, and 4) that the office he was seeking would affect the lives of Illinois citizens for generations.

The themes of a campaign should be expressed visually as well as verbally. While one exercises only limited control over the type of coverage given your campaign by the media, you do have complete control over the image created by your own buttons, brochures, and posters. It is important, therefore, to make a careful selection of visual themes early and to continue them throughout the campaign for maximum effect. The choices include questions of color, the typeface to be used for the candidate's name, photographs, and overall design. In making these decisions about visual themes several rules apply:

1. Keep it simple
2. Emphasize the candidate's name
3. Make all campaign materials easily identifiable
4. Make it distinctive but not wild

In the Weisberg campaign they decided upon orange background and black type, chose a Helvetica typeface which was slightly modified by the artist for the candidate's name, and selected a very high-contrast photograph. Taken together, these elements conveyed the image of a dignified but imaginative candidate and campaign.

Publicity

There are two important restrictions involved in the battle to gain maximum publicity for your candidate. First, the publicity effort must be an integral part of the entire campaign and not simply a side

⊗Bernard Weisberg

For the Illinois Constitutional Convention ANSWERS YOUR QUESTIONS

He fought Paul Powell for Fair Election Practices and Won

"Bernard Weisberg played the major role in making sure that the citizens of Illinois are able to select their delegates through truly non-partisan elections conducted without favoritism. Already the citizens of Illinois have benefitted from his experience as a constitutional lawyer... He has all the qualifications for most constructive and significant service in the Convention."

Adlai E. Stevenson III

Non-Partisan General Election
Tuesday, November 18th
You may vote for two candidates on November 18th.
You do not have to declare your party.

WHY DO WE NEED A NEW CONSTITUTION?

Because our present constitution is an archaic, outmoded document, written 100 years ago by and for a predominantly rural state of 2½ million people. Thomas Jefferson and our forefathers wrote a federal constitution for the ages: the state constitution was framed by short-sighted men. Illinois, the fourth largest state in the Union deserves better. That's why the voters decided last November to do something about it.

HOW IMPORTANT IS A STATE CONSTITUTION, ANYWAY?

You may not realize it but the state constitution seriously affects your life and your children's future well-being. The quality and financing of your schools are at stake... the taxes you pay to keep government functioning... justice and honesty in the courts... your precious rights and liberties under the law... the air you breathe and the water you drink... your right to vote. These are just a few of the crucial phases of your life touched by the state constitution.

WHO WILL WRITE IT?

That's up to you. Two delegates will be selected from each of the 58 senatorial districts in a "non-partisan" election. Here in the 11th district, I am your independent candidate. I am not bound by party politics or special interests. My only commitment is to you, the people of this community and the high principles you want advanced in the Illinois constitution.

Bernard Weisberg and campaign volunteer Rose Ratner in front of the Weisberg headquarters, a former movie theatre at 719 W. Sheridan Rd.

Walking tours throughout the district help Bernie meet hundreds of residents of Uptown, Lakeview, and Belmont Harbor.

WHY ARE YOU RUNNING FOR OFFICE, MR. WEISBERG?

For too long we have let politicians run our lives. The new constitution is too important to be left to partisan politics and special interest groups. I am a constitutional lawyer, I have argued cases before the Illinois and U. S. Supreme Courts. I was law clerk to Supreme Court Justice Tom C. Clark. But, equally important... I am a husband and father, and I live in this district, which is among the most diverse and challenging in our city. I care about this community, ALL the people in it, and I believe I can represent you effectively.

WHAT WOULD YOU LIKE TO SEE IN THE NEW CONSTITUTION?

I would like an uncomplicated and enduring document, like the federal constitution. One that people can understand. It must be flexible enough to serve the future and at the same time meet our present needs. I believe some of our most pressing needs are:

Modernization of the revenue article to permit fair but adequate taxes

Judicial reforms to take the selection of judges out of the hands of party politicians

Provisions to protect us from partisan manipulation of election machinery

Easing the overly difficult requirement for amending the constitution

Provisions to encourage more qualified men and women to participate in state and local government as candidates and voters

A more effective Bill of Rights.

Belmont Harbor is a favorite picnic spot for the Weisbergs... Joseph, Bernie, Jacob and Lois.

Alderman Bill Singer and Bernie talk to voters on an early morning campaign tour of Sheridan Rd. bus stops.

WHY DID YOU SUE SECRETARY OF STATE PAUL POWELL?

To fight on behalf of all candidates and the voters for fair election procedures and to lay the groundwork for reforms that will guard against partisan favoritism by officials in charge of our election machinery.

We won the first battle... there is a great deal more to do.

ELECT BERNARD WEISBERG DELEGATE 11th DISTRICT AND WE'LL BEGIN.

The 11th District comprises
Lakeview, Belmont Harbor & Uptown

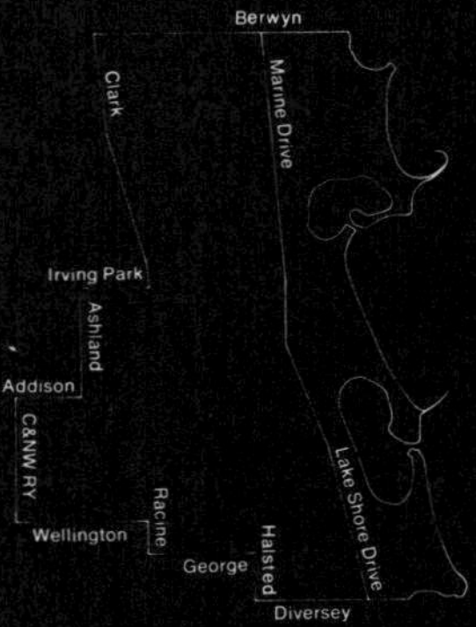

BERNARD WEISBERG

is supported by a Citizens Committee of more than 1000 of your neighbors and other prominent citizens.

Chairman
Donald Page Moore

Co-Chairmen
Dr. Preston Bradley
Rabbi Seymour J. Cohen
Mrs. Gloria Garcia
Stanley A. Kaplan
Rev. Adalbert Kretzmann
Rev. G. M. Kubose
Rev. Carl Lezak
Lawrence M. Mages
Dr. Marvin Rosner
Joseph Sander
Harry Vollen
Albert P. Weisman
Morton P. Weisman

Endorsed by:
Rep. Robert Mann
Cong. Abner J. Mikva
Ald. William Singer
Better Government Association
Independent Voters of Illinois
Independent Democratic Coalition
Independent Precinct Organization
United Auto Workers Region 4
Illinois State AFL-CIO

Chicago Daily News
Chicago Sun Times
Chicago Today

Citizens for Weisberg
719 Sheridan Rd. Chgo., Ill. 60613
929-0755

designed by Frank Reckitt
photos by Jim Taylor

ELECT

⊗Bernard Weisberg

TO THE ILLINOIS CONSTITUTIONAL CONVENTION.

I believe we all have a strong interest in assuring fairness at every stage of the governmental process. We should resist the easy lapse into cynicism—the attitude that this is the "system" and we can't do anything about it.

We can. This is why I am running for delegate to the Illinois Constitutional Convention.

Bernard Weisberg

Nonpartisan Primary Election
Tuesday, September 23rd

". . . MANY LAWYERS RECOGNIZE BERNARD WEISBERG'S SPECIAL TALENTS IN THE FIELD OF CONSTITUTIONAL LAW, AND THE VOTERS OF THE 11TH SENATORIAL DISTRICT ARE FORTUNATE, INDEED, TO HAVE HIM AS A CANDIDATE."

—William S. Singer, Alderman, 44th Ward

WHAT ARE BERNARD WEISBERG'S SPECIAL TALENTS?
Bernard Weisberg is a lawyer. He specializes in constitutional law and in cases that protect the civil liberties of all citizens. He has participated in landmark decisions before the United States Supreme Court.

He is a member of the American Bar Association, the Committee for an Effective City Council, the Committee on Illinois Government, and the board of Hull House, Jane Addams Center.

". . . OUR ILLINOIS CONSTITUTION HAS AN IMMEDIATE EFFECT ON ALL OUR LIVES. I AM GLAD FOR MY CHILDREN'S SAKE AS WELL AS MINE THAT BERNARD WEISBERG IS WILLING TO ACCEPT THE RESPONSIBILITY OF REWRITING IT."

—Congressman Abner J. Mikva

HOW WILL IT AFFECT OUR LIVES?
A new constitution can help put an end to unfair taxation—corruption in the courts—air and water pollution—poor quality education—and many other disturbing problems that destroy the quality of city life.

Bernard Weisberg knows this. His independence and readiness to fight injustice have already brought him the endorsement of the Independent Voters of Illinois, Independent Precinct Organization, Independent Democratic Coalition.

Citizens for Weisberg 719 W. Sheridan Rd. Chicago, Illinois 60613
Donald Page Moore, Chairman. Dr. Preston Bradley, Co-Chairman.
929-0755

activity in the hands of a single specialist. Publicity and the art of communicating through the use of various mass media are simply another way of recruiting workers and winning votes. Major publicity decisions, basic to the campaign as a whole, will often involve the entire campaign leadership because there cannot be one set of campaign themes and another set of public relations themes. The best campaigns will have unified themes which are then developed and exploited by publicity as well as by other campaign efforts.

Secondly, in developing a publicity campaign the single most important asset, in addition to a worthy candidate, is good judgment as to the newsworthiness of any event or announcement. News worth only a column note should not be sent as a major press release. Press conferences should not be called when an exclusive interview with a single reporter is more appropriate. Information developed for internal use or for direct contact with the voters may be inappropriate for public announcements. The publicity effort in a campaign thus involves a series of careful judgments as to what information is worth communicating, to whom, through what media, and when. Information about stupid things your opponent has said or marvelous things your candidate has done must be carefully released in ways that will have the maximum impact in building your campaign, communicating its purpose and character and, most of all, winning on election day. Without a thorough knowledge of the peculiarities and potential of each media, without experience with what the media considers worthy of coverage, these judgments will be hard to make. This is one reason that the advice of a professional public relations expert is important to a campaign.

As one example of a communications tool, the press conference is especially useful because it allows television and radio coverage of your candidate. But remember that unless your candidate is the incumbent governor or President, coverage will be limited. In some campaigns you may never develop news sufficient to call a legitimate press conference. In most major cities, where the large number of simultaneous campaigns makes the battle for media attention fierce, one or two well-covered news conferences are all that can be expected. As to the details of calling a press conference, a simple memo on campaign stationery telling the time, place, and purpose of the conference is sufficient. In major cities this same information also goes out on the news wire. Other than conferences which require a special location such as the opening of a headquarters, most conferences are held at a downtown hotel or, in Chicago, we frequently call them for the City Hall Press Room. After the memo has gone out, all of the major media are called and reminded of the conference. At early morning press conferences coffee and sweet rolls should be provided to the press who come.

Independent campaigns are not won by press conferences alone. With hundreds or thousands of campaigns occuring simultaneously and with F.C.C. rules requiring equal time for all candidates, constant, on-the-spot coverage is impossible. So publicity chairmen must also rely on the more ordinary press release and interviews to keep their candidate's name in the news. The model press release used in the Adlai Stevenson III campaign for U.S. Senate is included so you can get an idea of the proper format for a release.

The public relations process begins long before the first press conference. In fact, it begins even before the first story is written on your candidate. It starts with a visit by the candidate and publicity chairman to the major news media, or at least with the political reporters covering campaigns. It is the job of the publicity chairman to arrange for these visits and to prepare a Candidate Information Sheet and official campaign photograph which will provide background information and a picture for future articles that may be written. After political editors and reporters have met the candidate and information has been obtained about their deadlines and news needs, a steady stream of press releases — usually two or three a week — begin to be sent to the media.

If a release is going to be used by the media, it needs to contain news. The best news is that *someone* did *something* — hopefully, something different. The following are examples of the kinds of stories printed about the independent campaigns:

Bernard Weisberg filed today a suit in Federal District

SAMPLE PRESS RELEASE

CHAMPAIGN COUNTY
CITIZENS FOR STEVENSON
COMMITTEE

July 15, 1970

For immediate release:

20th STEVENSON HOME HEADQUARTERS OPENED IN URBANA

Urbana, Ill., July 15, -- Joe Doe, Coordinator of the Champaign County Citizens for Stevenson Committee, today announced the opening of the county's 20th Stevenson Home Headquarters.

The newest Headquarters is located in the home of Mr. and Mrs. Jack Philips of 1413 E. Jackson Ct., Urbana. The Home Headquarters is designed as a neighborhood distribution point for organizing volunteer workers for Adlai Stevenson III, Democratic candidate for the U.S. Senate.

The Headquarters "grand opening" will be Sunday, July 18, from 2:00 - 4:00 p.m. The general public is invited to attend.

-30-

For further information:
Joe Doe
217-694-3215 (Champaign)

BIOGRAPHY OF BERNARD WEISBERG

Bernard Weisberg, 43, is a lawyer, and a specialist in constitutional law who has participated in landmark decisions before the United States Supreme Court.

Mr. Weisberg was born in Columbus, Ohio, on December 16, 1925. He attended Columbus public schools and Ohio State University and received his B.A. from the University of Chicago College, graduating with honors in 1945. During 1946-47 he served in the U. S. Army, and upon his return did graduate work in sociology and education at the University of Chicago until he entered law school where he was a member of Phi Beta Kappa and a managing editor of the University of Chicago Law Review. He was graduated cum laude from the University of Chicago Law School in 1952 and was elected a member of Coif honorary law society.

After graduation he went to Washington, D. C. where he served as law clerk to Justice Tom C. Clark, United States Supreme Court (1952 term).

Since 1953, he has practiced law with a loop law firm (as a partner since 1960) specializing in corporate and financial practice.

Since 1956, Mr. Weisberg has served as General Counsel for the American Civil Liberties Union, and in this capacity has participated in and supervised cases involving a wide range of constitutional issues. Since 1965 he has been a member of the American Law Institute's Advisory Committee for the Model Code of Pre-Arraignment Procedure. In 1960 Mr. Weisberg presented one of the principal papers at the International Conference on Criminal Law Administration at Northwestern University.

He has served as Chairman of the Chicago Bar Association's Committee on Civil Rights (1964-66) and as a member of its Corporate Law Committee. Currently he is a member of:

Chicago Bar Association -- Special Committee on Civil Disorders
Chicago Bar Association -- Committee on Civil Rights
American Bar Association
American Judicature Society
International Commission of Jurists
Lawyers Committee on Civil Rights Under Law
Committee for an Effective City Council
Committee on Illinois Government
Board of Directors of the U. of C. Law School Alumni Association
Board of the Hull House Association Jane Addams Center
Anshe Emet Synagogue
B'nai B'rith

Bernard Weisberg and his wife Lois have two sons, Jacob and Joseph, and two daughters, Karen and Mrs. Jerilyn Fyffe. The Weisbergs live at 551 West Stratford Place.

C I T I Z E N S   F O R   W E I S B E R G

719 West Sheridan Road   Chicago, Illinois 60613   Phbne 929-0755

> Court charging the Secretary of State Paul Powell has shown "political favoritism" in ballot placement . . . .

> Bernard Weisberg, speaking at the Belmont Harbor Yacht Club, charged election fraud in counting the ballots cast in the 11th State Senatorial District in the September 23rd Con-Con Primary Election . . . .

Once there is news to tell there are a few simple rules for writing a press release in the form most likely to be accepted by the media. Hank Parkinson in his article in *Campaign Insight* suggests doing the following:

1. Make sure the release carries a name and phone number in case additional information is needed.
2. Include release instructions. (Is the editor to hold it for a day or two or can it be used immediately?)
3. Include plenty of white space between the release instructions and the copy start so a headline or instructions to the back shop can be jotted in.
4. Keep the margins wide.
5. Double space. (Never turn in a release that isn't typed.)
6. Never continue a paragraph from one page to another. (Use the word "More" when continuing a story to the second page.)
7. Keep the lead paragraph under 30 words in length, and never use more than three sentences per paragraph.
8. End the story with the symbol: -30- (this is journalese for "The End").[19]

It might seem that an inexperienced volunteer could be put in charge of publicity. But public relations is more than just calling press conferences or doing news releases. Successful PR work results in the candidate being interviewed by reporters, appearing on TV and radio programs, and notes about the campaign appearing in society or gossip columns. Success requires, more than anything else, knowing members of the working press and, more importantly, knowing the way the press works. A professional public relations person is much more likely to have personal contacts and to know deadlines and normal press procedures. If you cannot afford or are unable to recruit a professional, then you will have to be satisfied with an amateur. With lots of perseverence and hard work he can make contacts, learn the trade and get some coverage, but it will be harder than it would be for a good, full-time professional in the field.

In trying to mount a "professional" publicity campaign do not overlook simple and natural techniques which can gain great exposure for your candidate. For example, in an independent campaign, it is nearly always advantageous to draw your opponent into a debate. Begin with simple debates in front of community organizations. Many groups, at your suggestion, will be only too pleased to hold a debate. After all, they have the problem of dull meetings to overcome and holding a debate is a public service rather than "taking sides;" your opponents will find it difficult to turn down the request of a legitimate organization. Debates are particularly useful in effectively reaching more conservative sectors of the community which tend to support your opponent. A comparison between your candidate and the opponent may well convert important community leaders and win you votes you would otherwise lose. Later, during the run-off campaign you can use the debate format with the single opponent remaining in the race to get TV and radio time to better expose both candidates to the voters.

Another source of free publicity that is often overlooked are letters to the editor. The candidate or campaign workers can write several letters to all the newspapers during the campaign which may be read by more people than the news or even the editorials. As with everything in a campaign, there are successful and unsuccessful ways of doing the job. For best results the Stevenson for U.S. Senator Campaign suggested that volunteers in particular abide by the following Do's and Don'ts:

Do's

1. Use the Stevenson brochure and other materials sent to you by the Citizens Committee as your reference

material.
2. Always be sure of your facts.
3. Always be polite and objective. An earnest, honest statement, with the ring of conviction, can draw respect even from those who disagree with its content.
4. Write your own letter, in your own words. *Make it brief, neat, and clear.* Get your point across, then stop. *The best letters run between 100 and 200 words, no longer.* Long letters will not be printed.
5. Sign your name and address.

Don'ts

1. Don't write hot-tempered letters, or engage in personal attacks on the editor, or reporters. Avoid extreme statements.
2. Don't mail any letter that is unsigned. If you can't sign it, don't send it.
3. Don't copy other letters. Organized write-in campaigns have no effect. They can be detected instantly.
4. Do not assert as a fact anything that you cannot document.
5. Do not attack the newspapers. They always have *the last word.*[20]

Before concluding the discussion of publicity in participatory politics, it is important to spend just a moment on the role of advertising. For local races most advertising is too expensive because the media are beamed at a much larger audience than the residents of your district. That means that you pay a lot for your ads, and yet the bulk of the readers or viewers cannot vote for your candidate. One way of overcoming this handicap is to advertise only in major neighborhood newspapers. Also, if you advertise on radio, pick the station(s) with the most listeners from your district and concentrate on numerous ten second spots immediately before the election.[21] By either narrowing the audience reached through the media or by limiting the period in which you advertise, the campaign can save money.

An ordinary campaign ad is a waste of money for an independent. Most political ads in newspapers look about like the ad on page 75. As with every other aspect of the campaign, imagination and people should be the hallmark of the advertising. Thus, in the Singer, Weis-

ELECT

JAMES B.

KARGMAN

ALDERMAN 44th WARD

Senator ADLAI E. STEVENSON says . . . . .

"The Citizens of your ward and the Democratic Party are fortunate in having a young man of your ability and experience available to represent them."

Congressman SIDNEY R. YATES says . . . . .

"I believe Jim will make a good Alderman. He has ability and determination; he is conscientious. He will do a good job for the people of his ward."

Senator ROBERT E. CHERRY says . . . . .

"The people of the 44th Ward are fortunate to have a young man of Jim's ability as a candidate for Alderman. He will be a concerned, dedicated public servant."

Representative JOHN M. MERLO says . . . . .

"The people of the 44th Ward will be ably represented in the City Council by this articulate, well-informed young man. He will speak out for all the people, the young, the elderly, the rich, the poor. He has my full support in this endeavor and I am proud to be part of his team."

Also Endorsed by . . . . .
CHICAGO FEDERATION OF LABOR AND INDUSTRIAL UNION COUNCIL
UNITED STEEL WORKERS OF AMERICA—DISTRICT 31
44th WARD REGULAR DEMOCRATIC ORGANIZATION

"FOR A BETTER AMERICA . . . LET US BEGIN IN OUR COMMUNITY"

JAMES B. KARGMAN

VOTE TUESDAY, FEBRUARY 23rd

ELECT **JAMES B. KARGMAN**

ALDERMAN 44th WARD

"I'm voting for
DICK SIMPSON
on February 23
because

He's a proven fighter for fair and honest elections.

Ruth Rettke
1253 W. Addison"

"I'm voting for
DICK SIMPSON
on February 23
because

The job of alderman requires a man of the highest caliber, not a party politician.

Bennet Harvey
3240 N. Lake Shore Drive"

"I'm voting for
DICK SIMPSON
on February 23
because

He's taken time to meet with me and my neighbors and understand our problems.

Sarajane Donely
1449 W. Addison"

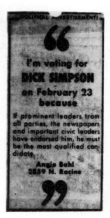

(POLITICAL ADVERTISEMENT)

"I'm voting for
DICK SIMPSON
on February 23
because

If prominent leaders from all parties, the newspapers and important civic leaders have endorsed him, he must be the most qualified candidate.

Angie Bahl
2859 N. Racine"

(POLITICAL ADVERTISEMENT)

"I'm voting for
DICK SIMPSON
on February 23
because

He is going to have a Ward Assembly where the views of all people in the ward will be heard.

Mario DeJuan
846 W. Barry"

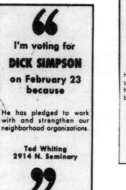

"I'm voting for
DICK SIMPSON
on February 23
because

He has pledged to work with and strengthen our neighborhood organizations.

Ted Whiting
2914 N. Seminary"

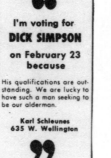

"I'm voting for
DICK SIMPSON
on February 23
because

His qualifications are outstanding. We are lucky to have such a man seeking to be our alderman.

Karl Schleunes
635 W. Wellington"

"I'm voting for
DICK SIMPSON
on February 23
because

He's shown that he has the courage to stand up against those who would deprive us of our rights.

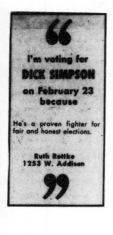

Mark Perlberg
612 W. Stratford"

berg, and Simpson campaigns simple testimonial ads were scattered throughout the neighborhood paper at modest expense but with maximum effect. These smaller ads were not consigned to a single section of the paper as with usual political advertisements, and because they were statements of real citizens rather than concoctions of a PR firm, they were read more often and their message was more convincing (see page 76).

Campaign literature

No matter what reception you receive from the mass media, you can distribute information to all the voters in the district by use of volunteers. There are, of course, several different types of literature, each with several different purposes.

To gain name identification and to encourage your workers, campaign buttons and small window posters are employed. Hundreds of citizens wearing campaign buttons are more impressive than hundreds of dollars of paid advertisements in the paper. And buttons only cost about $35 per thousand depending on the size of the order. Similarly, small posters have maximum effect when they go up in the windows of homes, for this demonstrates that citizens of the district are supporting your candidate — an impact that money can't buy. Some campaigns augment the posters with bumper stickers, car tops, and a special visibility campaign to put stickers on every utility pole in the district. Better financed campaigns even purchase billboard space; however, for most independent campaigns, buttons and small posters will create sufficient name identification and a good campaign image.

Getting workers to wear buttons is relatively simple and requires only mentioning the need for such visibility at all campaign functions. Getting hundreds of posters into windows is more difficult. A visibility chairman or team of workers must call every potential campaign supporter listed in the headquarter's files, asking that they put up a poster and get others to do so too. Posters are dispatched immediately by car to the homes of all who are willing to take them and a careful

Weisberg

TO THE ILLINOIS CONSTITUTIONAL CONVENTION

Pull Lever 3A

General Election Tuesday, November 18th

record of each poster is kept on a map of the district. As posters begin to go up, special efforts are made to get them into the weakest areas of the campaign and into at least one home near every polling place in the district.

Since buttons, stickers, and posters are primarily used to achieve name identification and general campaign image, they can be very simple — perhaps containing only the name of the candidate and the office he is seeking. Literature used door-to-door and passed out on street corners must be more complete — supplying information about the candidate's history, his platform, and the groups and institutions endorsing his candidacy. The literature may also contain photographs of the candidate with his family, with prominent supporters, and with voters in order to tell the campaign's story visually as well as verbally.

In the Weisberg campaign the basic piece of literature (page 63) was organized around the kinds of questions voters were most prone to ask:

Why do we need a new constitution?

How important is a state constitution, anyway?

Who will write it?

What would you like to see in the new constitution?

Why are you running for office, Mr. Weisberg?

Why did you sue Secretary of State Paul Powell?

Whatever method of organization is used to tell about the candidate, his reason for running and the office he is seeking, the information presented will, of necessity, have to be brief.

The best method of distributing campaign literature is by precinct workers going door-to-door: talking to the voters, answering their questions, and learning their preferences. Even so, there will be some precincts in the district which are not covered by workers because of the enormity of the task. Those precincts should receive a blitz — volunteers stuffing mail boxes with campaign literature. An experiment attempted by Byron Sistler in Evanston, Illinois indicates that just stuffing mail boxes for a slate of candidates endorsed by the Indpendent Voters of Illinois did have an effect on a limited number of voters. He found that in precincts which were not stuffed an average split-ticket vote for six endorsed candidates was 6.1% of the total vote. The precincts he stuffed had 8.2% of the vote for all six. The difference, 2.1% of the total vote or about ten votes per precinct, was affected by the blitz. The results demonstrate why personal contact is to be desired, but also why blitzes are used in otherwise unworked precincts.[22]

Campaign schedules

As many as three schedules may be kept in a campaign: 1) an overall campaign schedule, 2) a coffee schedule, and 3) the candidate's personal appearance schedule. The overall or master schedule is divided into several categories such as organization, candidate appearances, publicity, and precincts. During the early stages, events may be listed monthly, but as election day nears, weekly and day-by-day scheduling becomes necessary. Scheduling is important because, with proper planning, costs can be greatly reduced (overtime and rush orders on printing can double costs), logistical and clerical support by headquarters staff and volunteers can be coordinated to provide the necessary assistance for all sections of the campaign, and each campaign effort can be prepared for adequately. The coffee schedule and candidate's personal schedule allow the candidate to be present to speak when he is needed *and* insure that his time is used to the utmost effect. For instance, a candidate can attend three to five coffees a night as easily as one, if they are scheduled properly.

A good campaign schedule is molded around the deadlines to be met (filing and voter registration deadlines, election day, and PR production dates) campaign priorities (debates vs. shaking hands at bus stops) campaign theme (a "concerned candidate" must make trips into the community, personally check on school problems, etc.), and the resources available (money and number of workers). In making your own campaign schedule you will want to be sure to include the thirteen steps listed in Table 3 which occur in every independent campaign. Of course, each campaign will have other steps as well, but these you will have to discover for yourself. An idea of a what completed schedule is like may be found in the retrospective schedule of the Weisberg campaign. The kind of calendar you distribute to the workers is more like the one used in my campaign (see page 83).

Table 3
THIRTEEN STEPS IN A PARTICIPATORY CAMPAIGN

1. Bringing together a citizens' committee and locating a good candidate.

2. Preparing a voter profile based on census, prior election figures, and public opinion polls.

3. Deciding upon a campaign theme, creating the campaign structure, and selecting key campaign leadership.

4. Announcing candidacy and releasing first publicity.

5. Beginning coffees and direct contact to raise funds and volunteers.

6. Opening headquarters, hiring full-time staff, printing buttons and temporary literature.

7. Collecting petition signatures to put candidate on ballot and influencing other groups' (including political parties') endorsements.

8. Planning and holding rallies, benefits, special events, and training sessions for workers; sending final campaign literature to the printer.

9. Canvassing to register voters.

10. Intensifying coffees, candidate appearances, and media exposure.

11. Canvassing to locate voters favorable to the candidate, stuffing mailboxes, and leafletting at supermarkets and at bus stops.

12. Scheduling and training election day workers.

13. Election day: leafletting voters on the way to the polls, insuring that voters favorable to your candidate remember to vote, and poll watching.

Questions

1. Why is the image of an independent candidate as a "man of the people" fighting a political machine usually stressed? How does it help to accomplish three functions of public relations in independent politics? pp. 57-58.

2. What are some of the choices that must be made in selecting visual themes? Verbal themes? pp. 59-62.

3. What is the best kind of news for getting a news release printed? pp. 69, 71.

4. Why is the advice of a professional public relations expert necessary? Why can't just any volunteer do the job? pp. 71-73.

5. What are some of the ways that the cost of advertising can be lowered and made more effective at the same time? Also, of what use are debates and letters to the editor in a publicity campaign? p. 73-74, 77.

6. Which campaign literature is used primarily to gain name identification and to encourage workers and which campaign literature is meant to convince voters? How is the latter best distributed? pp. 77-80.

7. What factors most influence the campaign schedule? pp. 80-81.

Elect
Dick Simpson
your 44th Ward Alderman for
a
Happy New Year
Feliz Año Nuevo
Ake Mashite te Omede to Gozaimasu
Ein gluckliches Neues Jahr
Shanah Tovah
Bonne Annee
Citizens for Simpson.
1045 West Belmont • Chicago, Illinois 60657
stamp

Plan
Ahead for
Dick Simpsor
Election in 1971
January s m t w th f s
1 2
3 4 5 6 7 8 9
10 11 12 13 14 15 16
17 18 19 20 21 22 23
24 25 26 27 28 29 30
31
Tues. Jan. 5
Training Session
Registration Day
Workers
8 PM, Headquarters
Sun. Jan. 17
Last day to turn in
Change of Address
Cards
All day until 10 PM
Mon. Jan. 25
Precinct Registration
Polls open
8 AM to 8 PM
save this
space; add
events as
scheduled
February s m t w th f s
1 2 3 4 5 6
7 8 9 10 11 12 13
14 15 16 17 18 19 20
21 22 23
Mon. Feb. 1
Training Session for
Voters' Canvass
8 PM Headquarters
Sat. Feb. 6
Benefit Party
Time & Place
To be announced
Fri. Feb. 12
Lincoln's Birthday
Public Forum
Important: Fill this in
Phone Simpson Headquarters 525-6034
My precinct is
My polling place is
Sat. Feb. 20th
44th Ward Day
Gala Neighborhood
Celebration
Sun. Feb. 21
Training Session
All Election Day
Workers
11 AM Headquarters
Tues. Feb. 23
Election Day
Vote for Dick Simpson
Set aside day to
work at polls.
Polls open
6 AM to 6 PM
save this
space; add
events as
scheduled
44th Ward
Headquarters
1045 W. Belmont
Grace
Racine
Halsted
Cornelia
Lake Shore Drive
Southport
Addison
Ravenswood
C & NW RR
Diversey
Broadway
Wellington
Oakdale
Burling

Workshop Exercise

To make sure that you have mastered the ideas involved in publicity efforts and scheduling, divide into small discussion groups, choose a mythical or real independent candidate running for a local office, and attempt the following:

1. Decide upon explicit or implicit verbal themes for the campaign.

2. Make a rough sketch of a possible button and basic piece of literature for the campaign, being especially sensitive to the choices of color, typeface, photograph, layout, and slogan.

3. Draw up a campaign schedule for the campaign. If the key dates are not known, use those of Weisberg's campaign for the sake of the exercise:

   Petitions due July 7-11
   End of registration August 22
   Primary election September 23
   Run-off election November 18

Chapter V

Preparing For Battle

Staffing a precinct structure with leaders and trained workers able to effectively carry out a petition drive, registration campaign, and door-to-door voter canvass is the secret of winning on election day. After a precinct structure has been established, the petition drive allows a test of its efficiency and the registration drive allows the campaign to enlarge the constituency of voters likely to be favorably disposed toward your candidate.

Precinct work is what wins or loses campaigns. You can have the best candidate in the nation, good publicity, lots of money and successful campaign events, but if you lack the workers to go door-to-door, voter-to-voter informing and convincing the voters, the campaign is doomed from the beginning. On the other hand, if you have a strong precinct effort, you will be able to overcome many other campaign deficiencies. To mount a successful precinct effort you need good leaders, a structure capable of coordinating all the workers, and good petition and registration drives to get things started properly.

Precinct work provides our most direct contact with voters. It gives neighbors a chance to talk together about the kind of men and women who should represent them. Translating campaign issues so that each voter can understand what the outcome of the election really means to him and his community forces precinct workers to bridge the gap between rhetoric and reality and wins elections by reestablishing trust and human communication. Precinct work not only allows the campaign volunteer to participate, but prepares the voter for meaningful participation on election day.

HYPOTHETICAL PRECINCT STRUCTURE

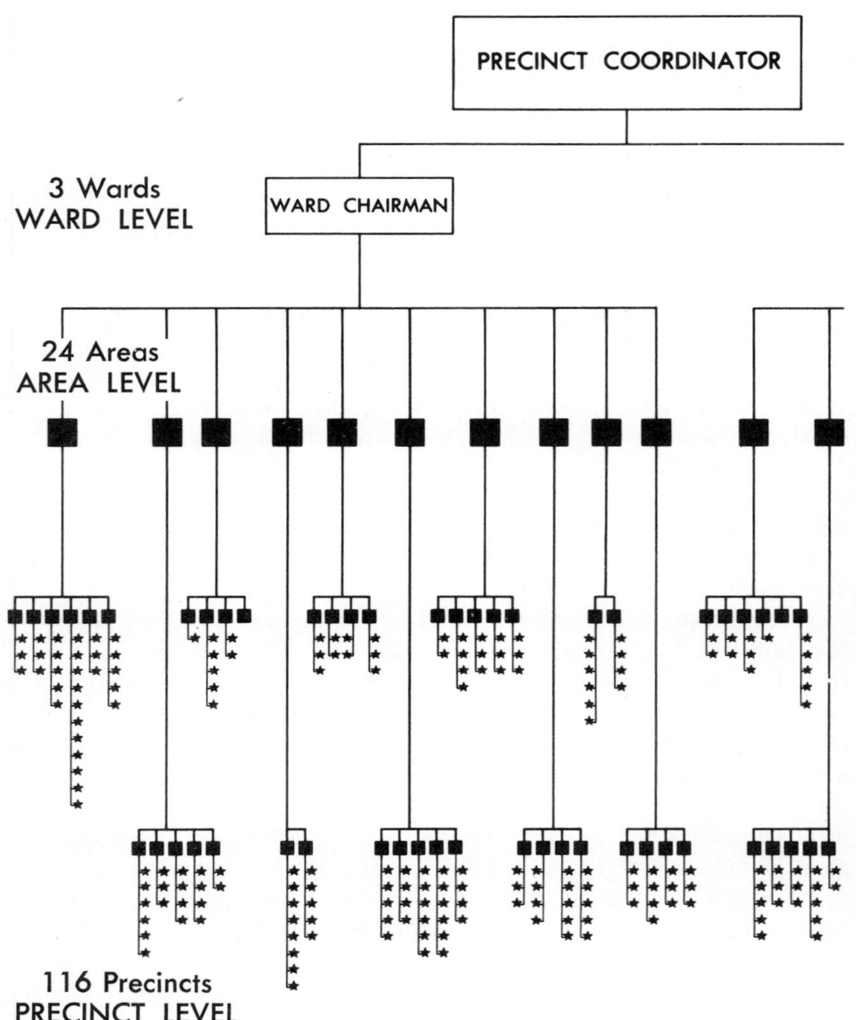

THE PRECINCT ORGANIZATION

1 Political Action Chairman
3 Ward Coordinators
24 Area Chairmen
116 Precinct Captains
402 Workers
546 People

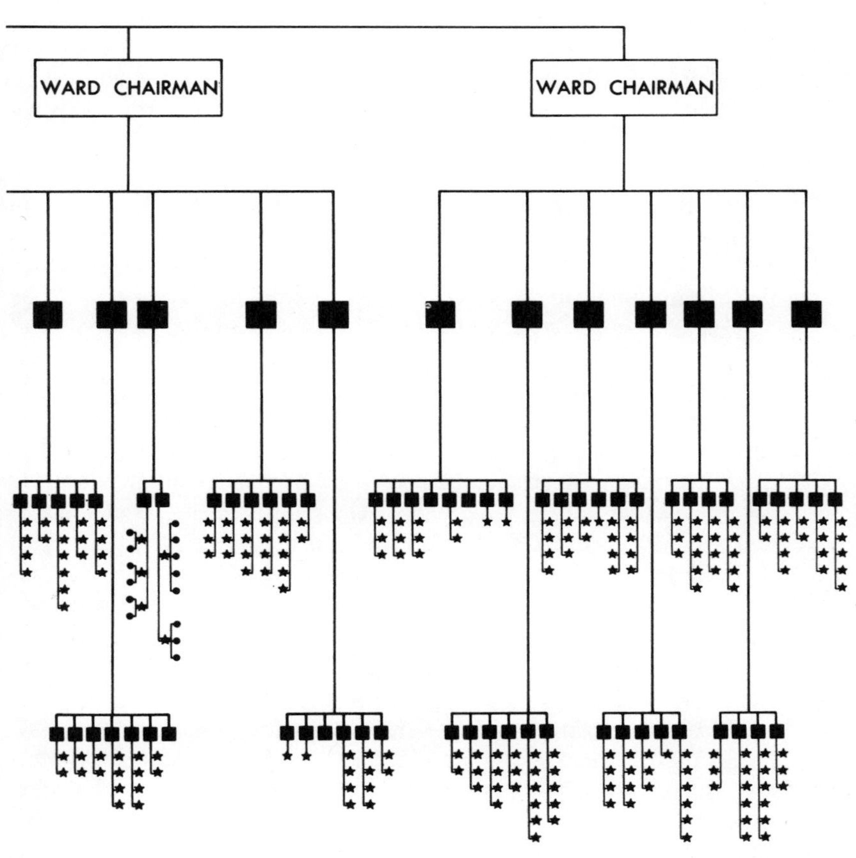

■ Area Chairman

■ Precinct Captain

* Precinct Worker

Source: Chart developed by Frank D'Alessandro,
Assistant Executive Director,
Independent Precinct Organization, 1970.

A precinct structure

Precinct work is so essential and the task so mammoth that it can be accomplished only by a highly structured and efficient organization in which each worker knows his tasks, does them well, and accurately reports the result. The success of the entire effort depends to a very large extent on the person who heads it, the precinct coordinator.

Several characteristics are desirable in a precinct coordinator. Like the candidate, he must be willing to give hundreds of hours to the campaign. If he cannot devote the time to do the job — most evenings and weekends for three or four months — then his other good qualities are insignificant. A good precinct coordinator also needs to be aggressive enough to get volunteers to do the hard door-to-door canvassing and hardworking enough to set an example for other campaign workers, but open enough to be able to communicate effectively with workers and to encourage constructive feedback and suggestions. Last of all, it is extremely beneficial if the precinct coordinator has prior campaign experience at least as a precinct worker. Locating favorable voters and getting them to the polls is the secret of success, and a good coordinator must understand this principle.

Because the precinct coordinator cannot personally supervise hundreds of precinct workers, ward coordinators and area chairmen are also needed. The responsibility for recruiting and coordinating precinct workers rests directly with these chairmen. Their duties require that ward and area chairmen possess many of the same qualities as the precinct coordinator. However, finding enough leaders is not easy. Sometimes precinct workers from prior campaigns can be "promoted". But some outstanding precinct captains make bad area chairmen because the two jobs require considerably different skills. A precinct worker goes personally to each voter. Campaign coordinators such as area chairmen spend their time on the phone convincing other people to work, giving instructions, and receiving reports. If experienced campaigners are not available or would be better as precinct workers, then you will have to make new workers into ward coordinators and area chairmen. You will find that some people are natural organizers or have professions such as that of salesman or business executive that suit them to the task; however, you always take a gamble in making someone a leader. Thus, the campaign staff must constantly check coordinators' reports and check with the people they coordinate to make sure they do their job properly.

Once volunteers have been found to serve in the critical middle management positions such as area chairmen it is extremely important that they be made to feel a part of the decision-making process. Weekly leadership meetings are centered around the area chairmen's reports of progress in the precincts, their suggestions for changes in strategy, and their reactions to proposals by other leaders. The candidate himself should attend the weekly meetings for at least half an hour. He cannot stay the entire meeting because it would inhibit discussion and keep him from meetings with potential voters and workers. But each week the candidate should report his perspective on the state of the campaign to the leadership and receive ideas from them. In addition to the leadership meetings (which cannot be matched for developing loyalty, enthusiasm, and full discussion of the campaign) frequent letters should be sent to the campaign leadership detailing accomplishments to date, the goals of the next leadership meeting, and instructions on the next phase of the campaign. Frequent communications should be sent to all campaign workers — particularly precinct workers. Many campaigns accomplish this by sending a regular campaign newsletter. However, it takes a lot of time to put such a newsletter together; an occasional letter about the campaign, along with invitations to attend precinct work training sessions may be sufficient. Finally, area chairmen should be encouraged to schedule parties and special worker meetings for those campaigners living within a particular area in order to further develop the spirit necessary to motivate people to do all the hard work they have to do.

Thus, a good precinct structure is much more than a chart at campaign headquarters. It is a large group of people working together and constantly talking about their work together. The personalities, personal concerns, enthusiasm, and loyalty of the leaders and workers can be more critical to the election results than the abstract description of roles they are supposed to play. Any successful structure must be flexible enough to take advantage of the unique abilities of its members, and their sense of participation and involvement must be fostered at every opportunity.

Locating several hundred precinct workers to fill out the precinct structure may be the most difficult task of all. The existence of permanent independent political organizations or a history of independent campaigns in your district makes a significant difference because they can be a major source of experienced precinct workers. New volunteers must also be recruited, but beginning with many of your precincts already covered makes it possible to concentrate on weak spots. To recruit enough workers you must hold many meetings, schedule hundreds of coffees, and call every potential worker whose name is given to the campaign. No campaign begins and few campaigns end with enough volunteers. Ideally, there should be three or more workers in every precinct in the district. Yet in the Weisberg campaign more than 450 precinct workers would have been needed. In reality only 85 of the 148 precincts had been worked at all by the September primary, and the total reached only 125 by the November election. The remaining 23 were "blitzed" with literature. Not even the best-run campaigns achieve perfect precinct coverage; but the more precincts you are able to work, the more likely you are to win.

Political campaigns always face the reality of scarce resources — too few volunteers, too little money, not enough time to get the job done. Thus, decisions must be made about the most effective apportionment of resources. Particularly in the deployment of precinct workers, there are two competing principles":

1. Try to cover the maximum number of precincts possible.

2. Try to cover completely the precincts with the greatest potential vote for your candidate. (The rule often quoted is, "Go hunting where the ducks are.")

Both principles are absolutely correct and neither can be ignored without jeopardizing victory. In the campaign for McCarthy delegates in 1968, twenty-two candidates were run in Illinois in almost as many districts. Only two were elected. In the 9th Congressional District the McCarthy for President campaign tried to cover over 500 precincts and only managed to get twenty percent of the total vote. Attempting to cover all districts and all precincts within those districts was a bigger job than the McCarthy campaign organization was able to handle. More selective coverage would have brought better results. On the other hand, in November 1968 Robert Friedlander, an Independent Republican candidate for State Senate in the 12th State Senatorial District of Illinois, wrote off thirty-eight precincts in the near north black ghetto. The Friedlander campaign concentrated instead on Republican and potentially independent precincts. He lost 30,000 to 27,000. Some of the precincts he failed to work contributed votes of 400 to 10 against him. While many Republicans and Independents voted for him, they did not turn out in the hoped-for numbers and the ethnic Democratic vote killed his chances of victory.

Worker placement must strike a balance between the two principles. You must try to cover every precinct in the district at least sufficiently to neutralize some of the voters and to reverse the proportion by which you lose from 40-1 to, say, 5-1. On the other hand, your strongest precincts have to be worked well so as to get as many votes as possible. That means covering a number of weak precincts thinly and concentrating manpower on your best precincts. As an added complication, you will have most luck in getting volunteers by letting them work the precinct where they live, so most of your volunteers must be left in their own precincts and only your best workers can be convinced to "carpetbag".

What should be done with large numbers of student volunteers if your campaign should be lucky enough to attract them? First of all, don't turn them away for fear of a backlash vote. While there may be anti-student sentiments in your district, they will be primarily directed against student demonstrators and revolutionaries, not against the young man or woman who comes to the door on behalf of a political candidate:

> The Movement for a New Congress' postelection poll in New Jersey's Middlesex County reveals that backlash is directed more against student demonstrators than against

> students per se, and is of negligible importance as regards student canvassers . . . . Whatever their attitudes toward student protest in general, when asked what they thought of the idea of students becoming involved in electoral politics, 71% of those polled said it was a good idea, compared with 13% who said it was a bad idea and 16% who weren't sure . . . . Only 2% of the respondents said they would vote against the candidate the college students were campaigning for.[23]

The best use of student canvassers is 1) to supplement your existing precinct organization with individual students assigned to beef up precincts that are short on volunteers and 2) to send teams of students to marginal precincts where "you are strongest in potential vote but weak in organization."[24] In these areas students can canvass for votes and, while canvassing, can search for potential workers who can build up an indigenous precinct structure in your weak areas. After all, it is the voters of a district who are choosing their own representative and who must hold him accountable after he is elected. So outside workers try to develop the indigenous leadership in each precinct to take over the tasks of campaigning, then move on to help develop new precincts.

Finally, a precinct structure requires careful records. At the beginning of the campaign, lists of potential workers are obtained from independent political organizations and from previous political campaigns in the district. These lists are transferred to a potential worker file on 3 x 5 cards with the name, address, and phone number. At the top right-hand corner of the card the ward number, area letter (areas are lettered A-Z to avoid confusion with wards and precincts), and precinct number are written in. These cards are the beginning of a master campaign volunteer file which is kept in the headquarters. A duplicate file of potential precinct workers is given to area chairmen for their areas only. The area chairmen phone the names of potential workers to each precinct captain. Later, if the potential workers become precinct workers, the code PCW is marked at the top of the card so that other campaign workers do not call them from the headquarters in search of volunteers to help with their projects.

After the initial set of precinct workers are recruited, additional volunteers are signed up at coffees or respond to mailings with the pledge card shown in Chapter 3. These are also transferred to separate 3 x 5 cards in the master file. The file is also enlarged by the recruiting efforts of area chairmen and precinct workers. By the end of the campaign, the file may number several thousand workers, potential workers, contributors, and friends of the campaign.

In addition to the master file, the precinct coordinator, ward coordinators, and area chairmen will keep their own records, including names of precinct workers and reports for each precinct showing the results of each stage of the campaign, from the petition drive to the vote count.

Petition drive

Petition drives which meet the *legal* requirements to get your candidate on the ballot are not difficult. However, many candidates fail to get on the ballot, or if they do, gain no other benefits from the petition effort. Particularly in machine-dominated cities like Chicago, no errors can be allowed if your candidate is to be on the ballot and the necessary support is to be mobilized to win the election.

If this is your first independent campaign in a district, have your petitions printed by the same printer used by the regular party candidates. He will use the proper forms and, since petitions usually cost only about thirty dollars, this is no place to pinch pennies. Later you can experiment with cheaper printers when you have the expertise to do battle in courts, over the forms you use if necessary. Decide upon your candidate, begin the campaign early, and have plenty of petitions printed. If a minimum of five hundred signatures are needed on the ballot, plan to collect one or two thousand signatures — which means you will need at least two hundred petitions with room for twenty-five signatures each. Not every worker who takes a petition gets it signed. Many workers get only ten signatures. Some petitions get lost. So print a good supply of petitions to begin with and don't hesitate to print more.

The petition drive is important. You need the maximum number of signatures because a number of signatures gathered by volunteers can always be challenged on technicalities: voters did not sign their names the same way they originally registered, the street address was not fully spelled out, etc. You need as many signatures as possible to be safe. Moreover, signatures provide names of potential supporters and test the fitness of your precinct organization at this stage. During this period of the campaign you will probably be working out of a temporary headquarters — a supporting organization's office or someone's home. This saves money and since your candidate is not even officially on the ballot, it may seem premature to open a formal headquarters.

The materials which must be provided for a petition drive are minimal. Each worker should have a set of instructions telling him who can pass petitions, who can sign petitions, when and where the petitions must be turned in, when reports are expected, and information about the candidate. The worker should also have a poll list with the names of every registered voter in the precinct. In Chicago such lists may be obtained free of charge at the Board of Election Commissioners at City Hall and look like the one on page 97:

Areas of the country which are not as politicized as Chicago do not provide prepared lists of registered voters. In such cases, you begin the precinct effort by copying such lists from official records or records from prior campaigns kept by political organizations. Since the petition campaign will take about three or four weeks, lists of registered voters must be completed at least a month before the filing deadline.

Registration

After the warm-up effort with petitions you are ready to launch the registration drive, a particularly useful stage of the campaign because:

1. It gets workers introduced to citizens on a non-parti-

PRINTED PRECINCT REGISTER -- OCTOBER, 1969

PRECINCT

42 WARD

This printed list of qualified electors was prepared from the registration record cards in the precinct file of each precinct as corrected and revised by any and all lodging house affidavits and challenges filed pursuant to statute.

HARRY G. COMERFORD, Acting Presiding Judge, County Division, Circuit Court of Cook County

	W BLACKHAWK ST
609	GRANT MARIAN H
611	ADAMS RUTHIE
611	MANNING THELMA I
611	NEAL FLORIDA M
617	CHANDLER JOHNNIE
627	FURMAN MAE
627	FURMAN TIMOTHY J
627	NELSEN OLAF M
	N CLYBOURN AVE
1473	BOSTON JOHN H
1473	CONERLY FANNIE M
1473	CONERLY K C
1473	LOYD LEUETA
1473	ROBINSON CABLE
1473	TURRY WILLIE R
	W EVERGREEN AVE
630	ALDRIDGE AMICA
630	ALDRIDGE GWENDOLYN
630	ALLEN CARRIE M
630	ALLEN LESTER
630	AMOS DORA
630	AMOS ROBERT
630	ANDERSON CAL HENRY
630	ANDERSON JAMES
630	ANDERSON JEAN R
630	ANDERSON LEE ETTA
630	BAKER GERTRUDE
630	BAKER LOVIE
630	BATTIE ROBERT
630	BATTIE ROSIE
630	BENSON ELIZABETH
630	BENSON MELVIN
630	BENTON EMMA J
630	BRANDON BERTHA
630	BRANDON L C
630	BROOKS LILLIE M
630	BROWN CLARENCE
630	BROWN DORIS G
630	BROWN EDNA M
630	BROWN INEZ
630	BRYANT AMELIA
630	BRYANT CELLESS
630	BRYANT FRANK
630	BRYANT OSCAR LEE
630	BUFORD LAURA
630	BYRD WILLIE L
630	CENTENO AMADEO
630	CENTENO EMILIA
630	CHAPMAN GEORGIA
630	CHAPMAN LONNIE
630	CHILDS ELIZABETH
630	CLAYBORNE CHESTER
630	CLAYBOURNE BETTY
630	CORREA ESTANISLAO
630	CORREA FELIPA
630	CRISWELL ROSE L
630	CROOK CARRIE A
630	CROOK GENERAL C
630	DAVIDSON MINNIE LEE
630	DAVIS ANNIE MAE
630	DAVIS CATHERINE
630	DAVIS JOHN R JR
630	DAVIS LOVIE
630	DAVIS LYMON JR
630	DELK JULIA
630	DOBBINS JEANIE B
630	LAWLESS MABLE
630	LENO LUCY
630	LLOYD ALICE D
630	LMINGGIO BIRDIE A
630	LOCKHART LLODIS
630	LOCKHEART JESSIE M
630	LOFTON MARY
630	LOVE OSSIE LEE
630	LOVE SHIRLEY ANN
630	MARSH ANDREW
630	MARSH ORA LEE
630	MARTIN CLARENCE
630	MARTIN LOUISE
630	MCCRANIE ELVIRA
630	MCCRANIE WILLIAM LEE
630	MCGHEE EARL
630	MCGHEE JACQUELINE
630	MCLAIN LELA M
630	MCNEAL MARY
630	MITCHELL EMMA
630	MITCHELL HENRY L
630	MOFFETT GERTRUDE
630	MOFFETT WILLIE
630	MOORE ELBERT JR
630	MOORE MINNIE L
630	MOORE VINIE MAE
630	MOTON ESTHER
630	MURDOCK DOROTHY
630	MURDOCK EUGENE
630	MYLES JOHN JR
630	MYLES KATHERINE
630	NORTH RENEE C
630	NORTH THOMAS N
630	PABON GEORGINA
630	PABON ROBERTO
630	PARKS LOVIE
630	PARKS LOVIE EARL
630	PATTERSON MINNIE
630	PEARSON JOANN
630	PEARSON WILLIAM
630	PETTIFORD JEROME
630	PETTIFORD LORETTA
630	PHILLIPS LULA
630	PHILLIPS TELLIE
630	PHIPPS BETTIE
630	PORTER ANNIE L
630	PORTER ELSIE
630	PORTER GAYLE
630	REDFIELD ALLEN
630	REDFIELD JEFFREY
630	REEVES MURRIE DEAN
630	REGAINS GLORIA
630	RIVERA ANASTACIO
630	RIVERA ANGEL
630	RIVERA PROVIDENCIA
630	RIVERA TOMASA
630	RIVERS BERNICE B
630	ROBERTS JOHN E
630	ROBERTS VEDA E
630	ROBERTSON BEVERLY
630	ROBERTSON OLIVER
630	ROBINSON ANNA
630	ROBINSON FLORENCE
630	ROBINSON GEORGE
630	ROBINSON REUBEN S
630	RODGERS EUGENE
630	RODRIGUEZ JUAN
630	SABB GEORGIA MAE
630	SCOFIELD ROSIE LEE
630	SCOFIELD VINNIE
630	SHAW BINGMON
630	SHAW WILLIE R L
1340	ALMESTICA ROBERT P
1340	BATTLE LENORA
1340	BATTLE PERRY
1340	BATTLE WILLIE R
1340	BAYS BOBBY D
1340	BAYS DORIS J
1340	BENTON FRANCES
1340	BENTON J C SR
1340	BENTON OTHA L
1340	BEY RUTH C
1340	BINDER IDA R
1340	BLACKWELL WILLIE J
1340	BLOWN BONNIE
1340	BLUFORD FREDDIE M
1340	BOGAN EDNA E
1340	BONILLA GEORGE
1340	BONILLA LYDIA
1340	BOWEN LUCILLE
1340	BOWEN MADISON
1340	BOYD HARRY
1340	BRANDT LOUISE
1340	BREWER BURNEY
1340	BREWER IVELL
1340	BROCK MARTHA A
1340	BROWN EUGENE B
1340	BROWN LINDA F
1340	BURKE ELEANOR
1340	CALHOUN CHARLIE MAE
1340	CALHOUN DAVID SR
1340	CAREY CLARENCE
1340	CAREY KATIE M
1340	CARTER BERNICE
1340	CHILDS CORNELIA
1340	CLAIBORNE JIMMIE
1340	CLEMONS CHARLEZETTA
1340	COLEMAN BETTYE
1340	COLEMAN RICHARD E
1340	COLLINS FRED
1340	COLLINS HELEN
1340	CULON ROSA
1340	CORBIT JULIA BELL
1340	COUSIN HONESTER
1340	CROSS ROSETTA D
1340	DAVIS CARRIE
1340	DAVIS ELMER
1340	DAVIS J D
1340	DAVIS OTHEREAN
1340	DAVIS RUTHIE M
1340	DERAMUS KATHERINE
1340	DRONES KATHLEEN
1340	EDWARDS CARRIE L
1340	EDWARDS ROXIE
1340	EVERETT LEVANCE
1340	EVERETT LOUISE
1340	FAIR AUDREY L
1340	FAIR CARL
1340	FLEMING ADOLPHUS
1340	FLEMING CLAUDINE
1340	FORD EARNESTINE
1340	FRELIX EDWARD
1340	GIBSON DANIEL
1340	GIBSON SHIRLEY L
1340	GILL EMMA C
1340	GILL JOHN D ROCKEFELLER
1340	GRANT LEE
1340	GRANT MEDINAH
1340	GUNN PATSY LEE
1340	HALL DOROTHY
1340	HALL JOHN
1340	HALL MARY
1340	HANEY BARBARA J
1340	HANEY DONALD W
1340	MEADOWS HERBERT
1340	MERRITT EARLINE
1340	MILLER EARNESTINE
1340	MILLER EDWARD W
1340	MILTON LOUIS
1340	MURPHY LUCILLE
1340	MURPHY SAM H
1340	NETTLES WILLIE
1340	NICHOLS HENRY J
1340	NORALS ENOLA
1340	NORWOOD ROBERT
1340	ODEN CHARLES JR
1340	OWENS YVONNE L
1340	PADILLA JUANA
1340	PAGE ERNESTINE
1340	PAGE HERMAN
1340	PAIGE LULA
1340	PATTERSON LESTER
1340	PATTERSON LESTER JR
1340	PATTERSON MILDRED
1340	PELT LAURA
1340	PERDUE BARBARA ANN
1340	PETERSON BEVERLY L
1340	PHARROW ALONZO L
1340	PHARROW JENNIE
1340	PIPPIN DIANN
1340	PIPPIN SHERMAN
1340	POPE BONNIE MAE
1340	POPE WALTER
1340	POSEY LENA P
1340	PRICE EULA MAE
1340	PRICE WALTER
1340	RAMOS HILARIO D
1340	RAMOS ROSA
1340	REEVES EARNESTINE
1340	REEVES SAMUEL
1340	REGGANS EDNA M
1340	RICHARDSON FRANCES E
1340	ROBINSON BERNICE
1340	ROBINSON MILLER L
1340	ROUTE GEORGE
1340	ROUTE WILMA M
1340	SCOTT CAROLYN
1340	SIMS JEAN
1340	SMITH DELORIS
1340	SMITH DOROTHY ANN
1340	SMITH LLOYD J
1340	SMITH MARY LOU
1340	SMITH PURCELL
1340	SMITH THELMA
1340	SPARKMAN DOROTHY
1340	STANDORS WILLIE M
1340	STANTON JAMES
1340	STRONG JOSHUA M
1340	STRONG VERDA M
1340	TALBERT IRVIN
1340	TALBERT ROSIE L
1340	TANKSLEY EDITH M
1340	TATUM ANNIE LEE
1340	TATUM WALTER
1340	TAYLOR BERTHA MAE
1340	TAYLOR MARIE
1340	TAYLOR WILLIE L
1340	THOMAS OSCAR
1340	THOMAS ROSIE L
1340	TODD IRMA F
1340	TOWNSEND CLEMMIET
1340	TURNER ALBERT
1340	TURNER FLOREDA
1340	WARD ANDREW J
1340	WARFIELD STEVEN
1340	WASHINGTON EMANUEL

630	DOTSON MARY L
630	DOTSON QUENTIN W
630	DUNAWAY EDWARD ABLE
630	EARSERY BERTHA LUE
630	EARSERY WILLIE L
630	EDWARDS ALICE F
630	EDWARDS ROBERT L
630	ESTHER CARLENE
630	ESTHER ROBERT
630	FLEMING MARY J
630	FOSTER MINNIE L
630	FREEMAN DORIS A
630	GLOVER DELORES
630	GORDON MARY B
630	GREENE ELLEN L
630	HALL ANNA BELLE
630	HALL ANNIE M
630	HALL DEE M
630	HALL OSCAR
630	HAMMOND ERNESTINE
630	HAMMOND LEE ANDREW
630	HARPER MARLENE
630	HARPER OLIVER
630	HARRIS FRED LEE
630	HARRIS GEORGIA A
630	HICKMAN FRANKLIN V JR
630	HICKMAN JOSEPHINE
630	HILL BEULAH
630	HUDSON BETTY J
630	HUDSON ROBERT
630	HUDSON RUBY
630	JACKSON BETTY L
630	JACKSON JONNIE L
630	JACKSON LILLIAN
630	JACKSON NATHANIEL L
630	JACKSON PHILL
630	JEEKS GLADYS
630	JEEKS VINETTA
630	JENKINS BETTY J
630	JENKINS WILLIAM E
630	JOHNSON CLARA
630	JOHNSON LUCILLE
630	JONES BINNIE R
630	JONES CHARLES E
630	JONES EVELYN
630	JONES WILLIE L
630	KELLEY MARIE
630	LAMB AUDRIENNE
630	LANDRY JAMES E
630	LANDRY VELMA LOIS
630	SHELTON ELAINE
630	SIMMONS ANNIE L
630	SIMMONS ZEBDEE
630	SMITH CARRIE E
630	STAGGER JAMES HENRY
630	STAGGER LILLIE M
630	STARKS CHARLEY M
630	TAYLOR GEORGIA M
630	TAYLOR LILLIE
630	TAYLOR LUCILLE
630	TAYLOR MILTON
630	TERRY MARY P
630	TERRY RALPH D
630	THOMAS DELORISE
630	THOMPSON CALVIN
630	THOMPSON CARRIE
630	THOMPSON MAGNOLIA
630	THOMPSON WILLIE E
630	THURMOND BLANCHOLA
630	THURMOND JOHN D
630	TRICE FLOSSIE M
630	VANERSON ELEANOR
630	WADDELL BOOKER T
630	WADDELL RUTH
630	WADE ROSE
630	WALKER LIZZIE M
630	WATERS JESSIE LEE
630	WATERS WILLIAM
630	WELL ALICE
630	WHITE EDDIE
630	WHITE FLORA M
630	WHITE THERESA
630	WILLIAMS EDWARD L
630	WILLIAMS EMMA
630	WILLIAMS GRACE
630	WILLIAMS KATTIE MAE
630	WILLIAMS MARGIE G
630	WILLIAMS MARGIE G
630	WILLIS ARTHUR
630	WILLIS JOHNNY L JR
630	WILLIS SARAH A
630	WILLIS VERLINE
630	WINTERS HENRINE
630	WISE JANELLE
630	WORTHY ANNIE LEE L
630	WORTHY JOHN
	N LARRABEE ST
1340	ADMESTICA ROSALIA
1340	HARRIS BILLIE J
1340	HARRIS GENEVA
1340	HARRIS ROBERT S
1340	HASSEL DELLA
1340	HENLEY EUGENE
1340	HENLEY GEORGIANA
1340	HICKS RICHARD D
1340	HICKS THELMA
1340	HILL BENNY
1340	HILL INEZ
1340	HODGE EDITH
1340	HUTCHINS JULIA M
1340	IVERY J T
1340	IVERY VIRGINIA
1340	JACKSON ALICE
1340	JACKSON DORIS
1340	JACKSON WESTREN E
1340	JONES ELLA RENE
1340	JONES JOHNNIE
1340	JONES PEARL M
1340	JORDAN WILMA B
1340	KENNEDY ALBERT
1340	KENNEDY CATHERINE J
1340	KILLINGSWORTH ALMA R
1340	KING MARY ALICE
1340	KIRKWOOD MARY
1340	LACROIX ALLINE G
1340	LACROIX WALDO L
1340	LEE JOHN L SR
1340	LEMON ESSIE L
1340	LEWIS GEORGE
1340	LEWIS PEARLIE
1340	LINDSEY WILLIAM B
1340	LINDSEY WILLIE LOIS
1340	LOCKHART DORIS
1340	LOCKHART JAMES E
1340	LONGS CHARLIE
1340	LONGS MANULLA
1340	LUCAS FRANCELL
1340	LUCUS WILLIAM
1340	MALLETT SANDRA
1340	MARTIN JEAN
1340	MARTIN LUCILLE
1340	MARTIN THOMAS R
1340	MCCOY CHARLIE MAY
1340	MCINTOSH AMOND
1340	MCLAUGHLIN JEAN
1340	MCNAIR ANNIE
1340	MEADOWS ETHEL
1340	WASHINGTON LULA
1340	WATSON ALICE L
1340	WHITAKER ELEANOR
1340	WHITAKER PETER
1340	WIGGINS W M
1340	WILLIAMS CHARITY
1340	WILLIAMS CHARLES E
1340	WILLIAMS DOROTHY J
1340	WILLIAMS JEROLYN L
1340	WINSTON RUDY M
1340	WOOD OWEN D
1340	WOODS ARLEAN
1340	WORTHY ALBERT SR
1340	WORTHY DORIS JEAN
1340	YOUNG LILLIE
1434	BLOSSOM LEE E
1434	BURNS ROSIE LEE
1434	THOMAS ESNER
1434	THOMAS ROBERT
1440	BURNS CORDELIA
1440	FIELDS LAURA
1440	JOHNSON MARY A
1440	MITCHELL FODIE MAE
1440	STIGGERS MARY G
1440	STYLES LUCILLE
1482	JOHNSON CLARENCE
1482	JOHNSON SARAH M
1482	LEWIS MACIE
1482	LEWIS WILLIE
1482	PAXTON EMMA SUE
1482	WALTON KATHERINE
1482	WALTON MABLE R
1484	COLEMAN ANNIE RUTH
1484	PHIPPS KATHERINE
1486	COLEMAN ROSIE LEE
1486	COLEMAN SILAS
1486	COLEMAN WILLIE MAE
1496	DUDLEY RUTHIE LEE
	N OGDEN AVE
1469	SMITH JEANETTE
1469	SMITH OSCAR A
1469	TALLEY DOLORES C
1471	JACKSON ALBERT
1471	STANDOR ALEX G
1471	STANDOR EMIL J
1471	STEWARD JAMES O
1477	MCDONALD JOELEAN

The undersigned members of the Board of Election Commissioners of the City of Chicago certify that the names on this list are the names of all voters entitled to vote at the November 18, 1969 Constitutional Convention General Election in the Precinct as located on the top hereof and, according to the Election Code, this list is prima facie evidence that the electors whose names appear hereon are entitled to vote.

Chicago, October, 1969

Stanley T. Kusper Jr. Marie H. Suthers Francis P. Canary

san basis. People will be more receptive when you return to solicit their vote.

2. It is an opportunity to help eligible voters to register for the first time. The vast majority of the people you register will vote for your candidate on election day.
3. It is an opportunity to locate supporters and recruit them to help with the precinct work. Every worker you recruit multiplies the votes for your candidate.
4. It allows you to locate weak spots in the precinct organization and correct them before they cause you to lose the election.

The registration drive is an excellent part of the campaign in which to make use of workers from other parts of the city or state. These "carpetbaggers" can be used alongside indigenous precinct workers or to recruit indigenous workers in areas where you have none.

The Movement for a New Congress has estimated that there are between thirty and one hundred thousand eligible voters who are unregistered in every congressional district.[25] In every ward or state assembly district there are likely to be at least ten thousand voters who need to be registered. Obviously that is enough to swing the election. Every campaign ought to establish a registration goal and work to meet it. In the Weisberg election, precinct workers registered over seven hundred voters, and your campaign can easily do the same. *As many as three-quarters of the voters you register will vote for your candidate on election day, partly out of gratitude for the service you render in getting them registered and partly because they often register in order to be able to vote for your candidate.*

In registration drives there are two alternative strategies: 1) selective or 2) saturation registration. Since registering voters is more than a civic good deed — it is a vital component of winning elections — the choice between strategies must be based to some extent on the advantages of each method for the campaign.

The selective strategy is particularly appealing when your candidate is running on a party ticket in a general election, and you are backing only the candidates from one party. The best method of selective registration is to do saturation registration in those precincts which, based on past voting performance, are most likely to support your candidate.

In most independent political campaigns, however, a general strategy of saturation registration is employed. In addition to expanding political participation, past experience has demonstrated that most newly-registered voters are receptive to independent candidates. The existing political parties already have their game down pat. As long as they can keep the players the same, they stand a good chance of winning. Therefore, they would prefer that no one rock the boat. It is to the advantage of independents to start a real political battle and draw as many people as possible into the fight. It is advantageous for existing groups like political parties to keep participation low. If the fight stays small, one of the current parties will win. If the audience gets drawn in, then the outcome is in doubt. "It follows that conflicts are frequently won or lost by the success that the contestants have in getting the audience involved in the fight or in excluding it, as the case may be."[26] By the very process of registering new voters, you change the constituency of the district and give your candidate more of a chance to win.

There are two ways in which you can get voters to make the effort necessary to register:

1. To lower the costs of voting by making it as easy as possible to register and vote.

2. To increase the perceived benefits by convincing potential voters of the importance of the impending electoral contests.[27]

One way to lower the costs of registering is to provide potential voters with correct information about registration. Thus, to register voters you must first know the rules governing registration. The following rules apply in Chicago but may well differ from those in your own community:

1. To be eligible to register, a voter must be a U.S. citizen, eighteen years old, and have lived in the state for at least six months and in the precinct for thirty days.

2. Up to five weeks before the election a voter may register in person at City Hall between 9 A.M. and 5 P.M. on weekdays and between 9 A.M. and noon on Saturdays.

3. Up to five weeks before the election a voter who has been previously registered in Chicago, but has moved from his previous address may re-register by filling in the back of his voter's registration card or an Application for Transfer of Registration (Change of Address Card) and mailing it to the Board of Election Commissioners.

4. Four weeks before the election a voter may register in person at his precinct polling place between 8:00 A.M. and 9:00 P.M.

You have three jobs in a registration drive: 1) to delete the names of voters no longer living in the precinct, 2) to get previously registered voters to fill out change of address cards, and 3) to get new voters to register in person either at City Hall or at the precinct polling place. In none of these cases can you trust the voter. If he needs to re-register, have him give you his completed change of address card to take to headquarters. The staff will forward the change of address cards to City Hall, but many voters would forget to mail them on time. If a voter has to register in person, you will have to go back and remind him — most voters won't remember on their own. *Even on election day, it is your job to remind voters to vote. If you don't, as many as one-third will forget!*

Obviously the registration drive requires the coordination of a large number of precinct workers doing fairly exacting work. Many of them will not have worked in campaigns before. Therefore, a formal training session is required at which they can receive written instructions, hear an oral explanation of the registration drive, ask questions, meet the campaign leadership including their own area and ward chairmen, be encouraged by the large number of other people working in the campaign, meet the candidate for whom they are working so hard, and pick up the necessary registration materials. This kind of formal training gives the workers a general, intellectual understanding of their job and a certain degree of motivation. Such training sessions will be repeated again before the canvass and before election day. Each training session can thus be brief and focus on the job at hand at a particular stage in the campaign. The written instructions on the Weisberg registration drive are included on page 103 both as an example of the type of instructions which workers should be given and because they explain succinctly how a successful registration drive should be executed.

Precinct work, however, requires more than a general, intellectual appreciation of the task to be done. It requires ringing doorbells and talking to people. Therefore, area chairmen and precinct captains should supplement the formal training sessions with direct help for their workers doing precinct work for the first time. Whenever possible, someone with campaign experience should accompany new workers to visit their first few voters either during the registration drive or the canvass. Working with an experienced campaigner will help the new worker to understand his job, to know what to say, and to get over the hurdle of the first doorbell. After such "on the job training" the new worker is left with the confidence and experience to finish the task.

As Jerry Murray suggests in *By The People,* the real test of a successful registration drive is the number of change of address cards workers collect.[28] Deleting names from the poll list is relatively simple, but getting new voters requires talking to the citizens. The change of address cards are physical proof that the precinct workers are doing their job well. This is so important because all new workers are shy about pushing the first doorbell. If they get over that hurdle in registration, then they will do a good job on the canvass. If they don't overcome their timidity during registration, they will be of little help in the election.

To insure that the workers are doing the job, there are carefully timed report dates when the precinct workers tell their area chairman, area chairmen tell ward coordinators, and ward coordinators tell the overall precinct coordinator specifically how many change of address cards have been collected, how many names on the poll sheets are to be challenged, and how many voters must register in person in each

HOW TO REGISTER YOUR VOTERS

Registration is a vital part of campaigning. Most people who we register will vote for Bernard Weisberg on September 23. Therefore, it is essential that we do a first-rate job during our registration drive.

Look over your poll list. As you walk up and down the streets of your precinct, note which addresses have no registered voters. Knock on their door, introduce yourself, and tell them that you are a volunteer worker for Bernard Weisberg, who is a candidate for delegate to the Illinois Constitutional Convention in our district. Ask them if they are registered to vote. If they say they are, tell them that their name is not on the poll list and ask them to show you their Voter Registration card.

If they say they are not registered, ask them how long they have lived at their present address, and how long they have lived in the State of Illinois and how long they have lived in the City of Chicago.

If they were previously registered in the City of Chicago and have moved from one address in the city to their present address, fill out either the back of the Voter Registration card, or fill out a Change of Address card. Make certain that they sign it, and *Make certain that you take it with you!*

If they have lived in the State of Illinois since September 23, 1968, and if they have lived in Cook County since June 23, 1969, but were never registered in the City of Chicago, they must register in person at room 308 of City Hall. If they do not fulfill these requirements, then unfortunately, they are not eligible to register for the delegate election.

In your materials you have three different colored sheets. Make certain that the name and address of everyone who filled out either a change of address card or a voter's card is listed on the PINK sheet. Make certain that the name of everyone who must register in person at City Hall is listed on your YELLOW sheet.

Several people whose names are still on the poll list have probably moved since the list was published. List the names and addresses on the GREEN sheets of everyone who is still listed on the poll list, but who no longer lives in the precinct. You have two GREEN sheets. Please make certain that they are both filled out.

After you have gone through all of the residents of your precinct who are not registered, and after you have listed the names of everyone who should be struck from the poll list, then go to see all of the registered voters in the precinct. It is possible that someone has moved in with them who now will be eligible to vote. Or it is possible that one of their children has now reached the age of 21. Or it is possible that a voter has recently been married and that his wife must re-register at City Hall because her name has been changed. Any unregistered person who will be 21 years old as of September 23, 1969 must also register in person at City Hall.

Be sure to hand each person you talk to a piece of Bernie's literature. *But do not do any campaigning now.*

Registration is most effective when it is conducted on a relatively non-partisan basis. We shall have plenty of time to campaign in the precinct later.

All Change of Address Cards Must Be Turned in to Our Headquarters Absolutely Not Later Than Sunday, August 17, 1969.

Be certain to turn in one copy of your deletion list (GREEN sheet) into our headquarters not later than August 17.

In order to accurately assess how well our registration drive is progressing, we shall ask for reports Monday, August 4; Friday, August 8; Tuesday, August 12; and Friday, August 15.

We shall want to know: (1) how many Change of Address cards or Voter Registration cards have been filled out (2) how many people must register in person at City Hall and (3) how many deletions you have on your GREEN sheets.

We are counting on you for a top-notch registration drive. We know that you can do it.

GOOD LUCK!

precinct in the district. In the Weisberg campaign four report dates were set to allow for ample prodding of workers and complete information on the progress of the drive.

The reports and, particularly, the change of address cards turned in at the end of the registration drive are hard data about the effectiveness of your precinct organization. They should be carefully evaluated. In areas where you get no reports or only reports of deletions, you must either provide the area chairman with the names of more potential workers or the area chairman must be replaced. If few change of address cards are turned in, then something has gone wrong. This is the best time to strengthen your structure. If an area chairman cannot do the job, you can either make him a precinct captain, or, if the "demotion" would be too embarassing, you can keep him as assistant or co-area chairman. In no case can you continue to count on workers who were unable to produce any results during the registration drive — either they must be supplemented or replaced. Failure to do so means you will lose that area on election day and possibly the entire campaign will go down in defeat.

Community campaign

As immensely important as precinct work is to participatory politics, campaigns do have other dimensions. One critical activity is to build and constantly to enlarge the coalition of community organizations and groups who support your candidate. Unlike the regular party organization, participatory politics does not begin with the "balanced ticket"of ethnic names, but with candidates with the qualifications, compassion, and creativity to best represent their constituents. But any district is already divided by citizen affiliation with community organizations, ethnic groups, religious bodies, and social clubs. While the most important appeal in the campaign is to the individual voter by the volunteer precinct worker, appeals to these other groups are needed to bring them out of their isolation into the political arena and to make the resources and supporters of these organizations available to the campaign.

The community campaign is begun with the citizens' search committee which brings leaders of many of these groups together to discuss their common goals, to choose a candidate they can agree would help them achieve their goal, and to lay a foundation for the campaign. The candidate enlarges this original group into a full-blown citizens' committee of supporters. Then, the coordinator of the community effort compiles a list of other groups in the community and their leaders. The candidate begins a series of meetings with individual community leaders to get their suggestions, their complaints, and their support (to the extent that they will commit themselves.) Remember that many of these leaders have never been asked to support a candidate before. They will be flattered at being asked and, even if they refuse to make a public endorsement, they will certainly tell many of their group members that they were consulted by your candidate. At the second stage in this process your candidate should attend key community meetings, introduce himself and mention that he will be running for office. He should make it clear that at a future meeting he would like to appear, perhaps to debate with his opponents. Simply sitting through these community meetings can make a good impression and can inform the candidate of the kinds of issues with which these groups are concerned. The third stage in the community effort is to get a debate between all the candidates set up in at least a dozen community organizations. Careful preparation of your candidate, in addition to the knowledge gleaned from meetings with community leaders and groups, should allow him to win the debate before these now favorable audiences. After the debate, area chairmen and campaign workers should sign up as many volunteers as possible.

The effort to involve minority ethnic groups in the campaign is particularly important. In my own campaign we made a special effort to reach the Spanish-speaking community, and the results were quite rewarding for both the campaign and for the Spanish-speaking groups themselves. Latins have been generally ignored and without any representation in Chicago politics. I began by attending meetings and parties of Latin organizations and by meeting individually with Latin leaders. Next I appealed to the Lakeview Latin American Coalition at a meeting attended by leaders of various Latin groups. They decided to endorse me and they chose their own Latin coordinator. We held separate events for the Latin community, in addition to the other campaign events in which they also participated, and we developed special precinct work training sessions in Spanish. An important reason for doing this was to train Latins in the art of precinct work. This way they would be beholden to no one candidate but able to work for and elect anyone they wanted in their area. If I failed to be a good representative, they could easily run their own candidate. Last of all, we had special mailings in Spanish and special Spanish brochures for precinct work. In the case of minority groups, a candidate who wants their support must make an extra effort to reach them, and the campaign must be flexible enough to allow for a parallel campaign by minority campaign workers.

Questions

1. What qualities are needed in a good precinct coordinator? What is the likelihood of finding someone who meets all these qualifications? p. 90

2. What are two main principles of precinct worker deployment and how should they influence your campaign? pp. 92-93

3. What is the best use of student volunteers in the precincts? p. 93

4. What materials are needed to conduct a petition drive and what results should be expected? pp. 95-96

5. What are the basic alternative strategies of registration? Which ones do independents usually follow? Why is it to the advantage of independents to increase registration and participation? pp. 99-100

6. What are the functions of formal training sessions, written instructions and on the job training in precinct work? pp.101-102

7. Why is the success of a registration campaign usually measured

by the number of change of address cards turned in? p. 102

8. How can registration results be used to strengthen the precinct structure? pp. 102, 105

9. How is a community campaign run and what are its effects? pp. 105-107

Chapter VI
Canvassing the Voters

While campaign techniques may differ in wealthy and ghetto precincts, in urban and rural areas, in national and local elections, a careful canvass for favorable voters and getting those favorable voters to the polls remains a constant goal. The work is hard, the sacrifices are many, but the results on election day justify them.

The canvass takes place about three or four weeks before the election, and the function of this phase of the campaign is to locate all the voters favorable or potentially favorable to your candidate. A secondary, but still important, function is to "mobilize lukewarm supporters."[29] The importance of locating your voters was stressed in the written instructions given to all Weisberg precinct workers:

> Most people think of precinct workers as strong-arm salesmen. Actually, nothing could be further from the truth. The "sales" pitch is really a smokescreen to conceal the worker's true intent, which is to find out for whom the voter plans to cast his ballot on election day. Elections are won by locating and identifying the vote and, on election day, being sure that those voters who intend to vote for us actually do vote.[30] (see page 110 for complete form)

In practice, however, precinct workers affect voters, as well as learning their preferences, simply by providing information about the election and your candidate:

> . . . the issue content of the canvasser's appeal is far less important than conveying the most elementary facts: first, that an election is about to take place, and second, that the name of one of the candidates is the one you are working for.[31]

HOW TO WIN ELECTIONS

Most people think of precinct workers as strong-arm salesmen. Actually, nothing could be further from the truth. The "sales" pitch is really a smokescreen to conceal the worker's true intent, which is to find out for whom the voter plans to cast his ballot on election day. Elections are won by locating and identifying the vote and, on election day, being sure that those voters who intend to vote for us actually do vote.

Your canvassing material will include:

A precinct poll list
Literature
Buttons, stickers, etc.

Locating the vote:

1. Before you knock or ring the bell, make sure you know the names of the people who live there.
2. Introduce yourself. You are a neighbor and a volunteer for Bernard Weisberg, the Independent candidate for the Illinois Constitutional Convention.
3. Hand the voter the basic piece of literature and "sell" the candidate. About two or three sentences should be sufficient. If the voter wants to know more about Bernie, give him a Biography Sheet as you answer his questions.
4. Determine the voter's attitude by asking a subtle but sufficiently direct question. For example, "May we count on your supporting our candidate on election day?"
5. Evaluate the voter:

a. Mark a *plus* (+) in front of the voter's name on the precinct poll list if he is for our man.
b. Mark a *minus* (–) in front of the voter's name if the voter definitely will not vote for Bernie.
c. Mark a *zero* (0) if the voter is undecided or refuses to tell you.

6. Leave as quickly and as courteously as you can. *Never* argue.
7. Continue in this manner until every vote has been located and evaluated. If no one is home, leave literature and call again.
8. Don't fake. If a voter wants further information or asks questions you are unable to answer, note the question, ask your ward or area chairman for the answer, and go back to the voter.

In order to gauge voter response to our campaign, periodic checks will be made by your area chairman or precinct captain. You will be asked for a count of *plus, minus* and *zero* voters on:

Thursday, October 30
Tuesday, November 4
Sunday, November 9
Thursday, November 13

Work systematically. You should have:

One-third of the precinct completed by November 4.
Three-quarters of the precinct completed by November 10.
The entire precinct completed by November 13.

After you have finished your part of the canvass, return the precinct poll list (the *plus* list) to your precinct captain or area chairman.

Keep the weekend of November 15 and 16 open to deliver reminder cards to each "plus" and "zero" voter as well as to contact those voters whom you may have missed during the original canvass.

It has been said many times that elections are won in the precincts. Personal contact with the voters is the required ingredient for victory. You must realize that you, the precinct worker, will determine who will win and who will lose on Tuesday, November 18th. Good Luck!! Citizens for Weisberg, 719 West Sheridan Road, Chicago, Illinois 60613 Phone: 929-0755

Precinct workers are often able to let voters know what their candidate is doing about the issues which concern them—from mundane matters like street sweeping to ideological questions such as freedom of speech — and to answer questions the voter may have. You are, thus, the personal representative of your candidate. Many voters will judge the candidate by your appearance and by what you say. If they decide to vote for your candidate, they are in reality casting a vote for *you*, just as when they vote for your opponent they are often voting for his precinct worker. Because independents normally represent better qualified candidates and because they ask voters to decide for whom to vote on the merits of the issues instead of deciding on the basis of "favors" past or promised, they can beat regular precinct captains in most precincts. But it does take hard work.

After talking about your candidate, a voter's position on the election is determined by politely asking, "May we count on your support for our candidate on election day?" or a similar question. Based on the voter's response, you will mark a plus (+), minus (–) or zero (0) beside his name on the poll list, just as workers in the 5th precinct of the 44th Ward filled in the poll sheet in my campaign shown on page 113. When you are finished with the canvass you will have a list of *plus voters* who favor your candidate, *minus voters* who favor your opponent, and from one-third to one-half of the list who are *zero-voters* (would not say how they will be voting or have not yet decided.) Unless told differently by the voter, you can normally assume that all members of the family will vote the same way. Jim Chapman in *By The People* explained the system to the Weisberg precinct workers this way:

> If a person indicates to you, "Yes, I will vote for Bernie" on your precinct list, put a plus. If he says "No," put a minus. And if the person says "I really haven't made up my mind yet," you put down a zero. So that when we come to election day there is a system where we will try to reach these people, to call them, to go to their doors —

5	PRECINCT
44	WARD

PRINTED PRECINCT REGISTER — JANUARY, 1971

This printed list of registered voters was prepared from the verification book returned by the precinct canvassers after the canvass of January 27 and 28, 1971. The canvassers have certified that the persons whose names appeared in the verification book were qualified to vote from the addresses listed as of the time of the canvass. In addition to the names in the verification book the Board of Election Commissioners has added to the list the names of voters who registered or submitted requests for changes of address during the final period of registration when it was too late to submit them to the canvassers for the precinct canvass.

It is possible that some voter or voters whose names appear on this list may become disqualified by moving or some other reason before the day of election. Any registered voter who is a resident of the ward and who has personal knowledge that a person whose name appears on this list is not qualified to vote from the address listed, may file an application to have the name of said voter erased from the registry. This application must be filed in person in the Office of the Board of Election Commissioners on February 8 or 9, between the hours of 9 o'clock a.m. and 6 o'clock p.m.

HARRY G. COMERFORD, Presiding Judge, County Division, Circuit Court of Cook County

W PARRY AVE

417	BROWN TIMOTHY W
417	CERNIAK JACQUELYN F
417	CUSICK JEANNE
417	DILL BEATRICE A
417	FLANDRO CAROL L
417	FLANDRO CLAUDE S
417	FORBES JOAN E
417	GALLAGHER MICHAEL J
417	GOLDBERG JEAN
417	HINRICHS MARJORIE M
417	HUNTER HAROLD B
417	HUNTER LYNNE
417	JENKINS GERTRUDE G
417	KEYES JAMES F
417	KEYES MARIAN E
417	LONDRIGAN MARY P
417	MASON DIANA L
417	MASON MICHAEL E
417	MOHLMAN JEANETTE M
417	PACE JOANN A
417	PANTHER HELEN R
417	RANIERI KATHERINE A
417	ROOZ FRANCES
417	RUPPERT TOM R
417	SEITER BARBARA L
417	TRAEBER EMMY M
417	YOUNG LAVERNE
417	ZALLY BARBARA L
421	ADELMAN BARBARA A
421	ADELMAN BEATRICE M
421	BENDOV BARBARA L
421	BENDOV EITAN
421	CHENOWETH MARSCHA J
421	CHRISTIANSON STARR D
421	CLARK JANICE
421	CONNER NANCY E
421	CREBS BETTY LOU
421	CREBS MARIE E
421	CROWLEY KATHLEEN
421	DVORIN HAROLD L
421	FLOOD GRACE M
445	CARROLL EDITH
445	CROWLEY MIRIAM C
445	DANIELS ROBERT L
445	DAUGIRDAS GEORGE S
445	DAVIS KAREN V
445	DENHART KAREN L
445	DWYER JAMES G
445	ELSON KATHLEEN
445	ERICKSEN JOHANNA H
445	FIORINO MICHAEL
445	FIORINO MICHELE A
445	GOLDFARB HARRIS W
445	GORAVICA BARBARA
445	HEFTER PATRICIA E
445	HERBST MONA K
445	HILD FLORANCE M
445	HOLDEN RONALD S
445	HOSEK CHRISTINE M
445	HOWE RAYMOND J
445	HUNTER CHARLES J
445	IBRAGIC IDRIS
445	IBRAGIC MARIE E
445	JAMIESON JAMES J
445	JOHNSON KENNETH L
445	JUSTER MARJORIE E
445	KASPER KATHLEEN A
445	LANE PATRICIA E
445	LARSEN MEREDITH E
445	LEGG MAY A
445	LEVIN DONNA S
445	LEWIN ROBERT H
445	LEWIN SALLY L
445	MILLER ALLA
445	MILLER JOSEPH D
445	MURDAKES PETER
445	MURRAY ROBERT J
445	MYER CHARLES C
445	MYER RUBY F
445	NAGLE NOREEN M
445	OBRIEN WILLIAM M
445	PIENKOS ELOISE M
445	POLIDORI ROBERTA B
445	REARDON MARY J
3000	MCBARRON MARY P
3000	MCEVOY CHARLES L
3000	MCEVOY ROSEMARY R
3000	MCGURTY RACHEL
3000	METZGER ISABELL M
3000	MEYER EMILY
3000	MEYER JOSEPH C
3000	MEYER RUTH
3000	OLSHAN LARRY A
3000	OLSHAN SALLY A
3000	ORQURKE CECILIA M
3000	PENTONEY KEVIN J
3000	PENTONEY MARIE J
3000	PETERSON DOROTHY W
3000	PETERSON KENT F
3000	POWERS CHARLES J
3000	RAYNER ESTYL
3000	RAYNER HAROLD A
3000	REGAN JOHN F
3000	REGAN JOSEPH J
3000	REGAN MARY J
3000	RIGHEIMER FRANK S JR
3000	RIGHEIMER KAREN
3000	ROCCA JOSEPHINE C
3000	RODDA ESTHER R
3000	RODDA WILLIAM H
3000	ROSE LINCOLN H
3000	ROSE ROBERTA B
3000	ROSENBERG JEANETTE
3000	ROSENBERG SIDNEY
3000	ROSENSTEIN ELSIE D
3000	ROSENSTEIN MORRIS G
3000	ROWELL FRANK F JR
3000	ROWELL MABEL D
3000	SCHULZ MARGARET K
3000	SCHULZ SELLMANN C
3000	SCIARRETTA ESTHER A
3000	SCIARRETTA SYLVIO A
3000	SHAUGHNESSY ANN
3000	SHAUGHNESSY MARGUERITE
3000	STILL ANNE
3000	SILVER GERALDINE R
3000	SILVER JEROME M
3033	GILLESPIE RITA A
3033	GOLDE IRENE T
3033	GOLDE MARTIN J
3033	GORDON BETTY
3033	GRASS LORETTA D
3033	GREENBERG KATE
3033	GREENBERG WILLIAM
3033	GREENE NORMAN I
3033	GREENE SUSAN WITMER
3033	GROSS EDITH A
3033	HASTINGS DEIRDRE L
3033	HASTINGS WILLMORE C
3033	HEYER FRANCES W
3033	HLACH CONRAD C
3033	HODGES AGNES E
3033	HOLLAND TILLIE
3033	HRUSKA BETTY L
3033	HUTTNER DANIEL
3033	HUTTNER ROSE
3033	JACOBSON BLANCHE
3033	JAFFE DORA
3033	JAFFE SAM
3033	JULIANO CAROLE E
3033	JULIANO ROBERT E
3033	KANTER ARNOLD
3033	KANTER YVETTE
3033	KARP JANE B
3033	KELLER CATHERINE M
3033	KILIAN MICHAEL D
3033	KIMOTO RICHARD Y
3033	KIMOTO SANDRA Y
3033	KIPNIS LEONARD
3033	KOENIG BETTY
3033	KOENIG BETTY
3033	KOMAREK CECILIA M
3033	KORDA LOIS J
3033	KORDA STEVEN P
3033	KORSHAK MURIEL A
3033	KOVEN JOSEPH G
3033	KOVEN MARY
3033	KRISO EVA
3033	KRIZAK STEPHEN J
3033	KUSHNER IRVING

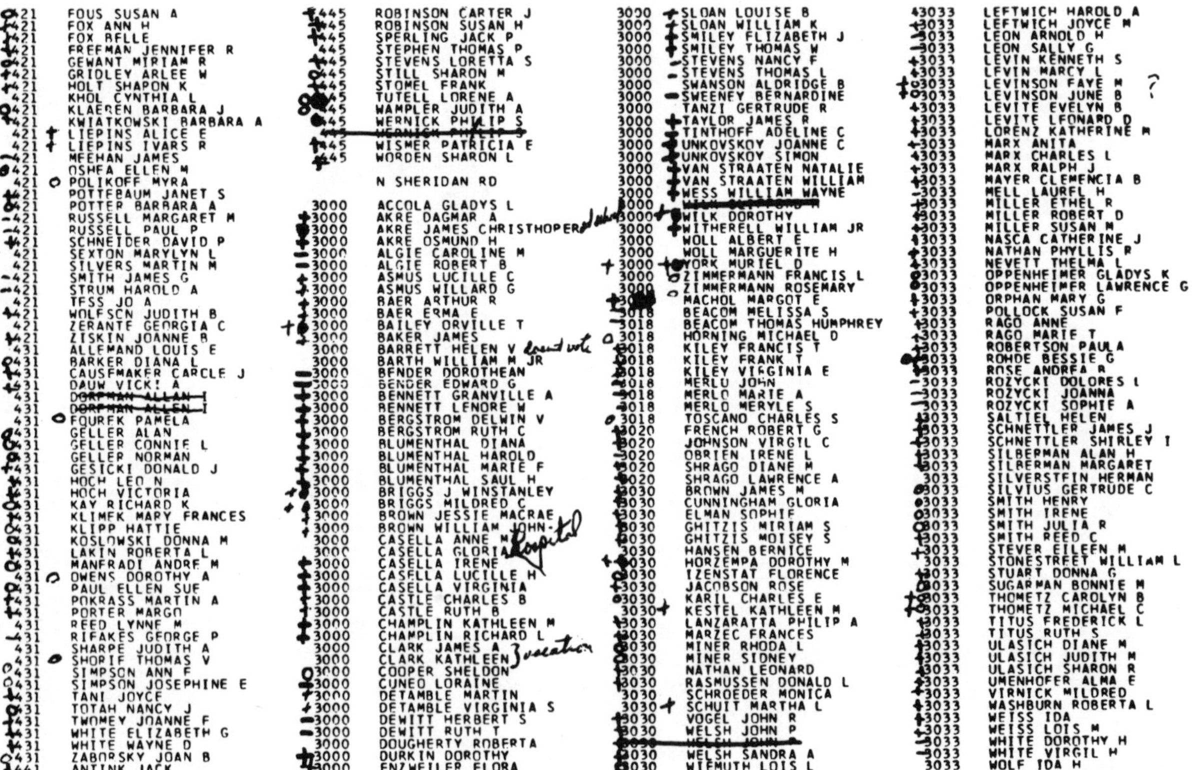

421	FOUS SUSAN A
421	FOX ANN H
421	FOX BELLE
421	FREEMAN JENNIFER R
421	GEWANT MIRIAM R
421	GRIDLEY ARLEE W
421	HOLT SHARON K
421	KHOL CYNTHIA L
421	KLAEREN BARBARA J
421	KWIATKOWSKI BARBARA A
421	LIEPINS ALICE E
421	LIEPINS IVARS R
421	MEEHAN JAMES
421	OSHEA ELLEN M
421	POLIKOFF MYRA
421	POTTEBAUM JANET S
421	POTTER BARBARA A
421	RUSSELL MARGARET M
421	RUSSELL PAUL P
421	SCHNEIDER DAVID P
421	SEXTON MARYLYN L
421	SILVERS MARTIN M
421	SMITH JAMES G
421	STRUM HAROLD A
421	TESS JO A
421	WOLFSON JUDITH B
421	ZERANTE GEORGIA C
421	ZISKIN JOANNE B
431	ALLEMAND LOUIS E
431	BARKER DIANA L
431	CAUSEMAKER CAROLE J
431	DAUW VICKI A
431	DORFMAN ALLAN I
431	DORFMAN ALLEN I
431	FOUREK PAMELA
431	GELLER ALAN
431	GELLER CONNIE L
431	GELLER NORMAN
431	GESICKI DONALD J
431	HOCH LEO N
431	HOCH VICTORIA
431	KAY RICHARD K
431	KLIMEK MARY FRANCES
431	KLIPP HATTIE
431	KOSLOWSKI DONNA M
431	LAKIN ROBERTA L
431	MANFRADI ANDRE M
431	OWENS DOROTHY A
431	PAUL ELLEN SUE
431	POKRASS MARTIN A
431	PORTER MARGO
431	REED LYNNE M
431	RIFAKES GEORGE P
431	SHARPE JUDITH A
431	SHORIF THOMAS V
431	SIMPSON ANN E
431	SIMPSON JOSEPHINE E
431	TANI JOYCE
431	TOTAH NANCY J
431	TWOMEY JOANNE F
431	WHITE ELIZABETH G
431	WHITE WAYNE D
431	ZABORSKY JOAN B
441	ANTINK JACK

445	ROBINSON CARTER J
445	ROBINSON SUSAN H
445	SPERLING JACK P
445	STEPHEN THOMAS P
445	STEVENS LORETTA S
445	STILL SHARON M
445	STOMEL FRANK
445	TUTELL LORENE A
445	WAMPLER JUDITH A
445	WERNICK PHILIP S
445	[illegible]
445	WISMER PATRICIA E
445	WORDEN SHARON L

N SHERIDAN RD

3000	ACCOLA GLADYS L
3000	AKRE DAGMAR A
3000	AKRE JAMES CHRISTHOPER
3000	AKRE OSMUND H
3000	ALGIE CAROLINE M
3000	ALGIE ROBERT B
3000	ASMUS LUCILLE C
3000	ASMUS WILLARD G
3000	BAER ARTHUR R
3000	BAER ERMA E
3000	BAILEY ORVILLE T
3000	BAKER JAMES
3000	BARRETT HELEN V
3000	BARTH WILLIAM M JR
3000	BENDER DOROTHEAN
3000	BENDER EDWARD G
3000	BENNETT GRANVILLE A
3000	BENNETT LENORE W
3000	BERGSTROM DELWIN V
3000	BERGSTROM RUTH C
3000	BLUMENTHAL DIANA
3000	BLUMENTHAL HAROLD
3000	BLUMENTHAL MARIE F
3000	BLUMENTHAL SAUL H
3000	BRIGGS J WINSTANLEY
3000	BRIGGS MILDRED C
3000	BROWN JESSIE MACRAE
3000	BROWN WILLIAM JOHN
3000	CASELLA ANNE M
3000	CASELLA GLORIA
3000	CASELLA IRENE
3000	CASELLA LUCILLE H
3000	CASELLA VIRGINIA
3000	CASTLE CHARLES B
3000	CASTLE RUTH B
3000	CHAMPLIN KATHLEEN M
3000	CHAMPLIN RICHARD L
3000	CLARK JAMES A
3000	CLARK KATHLEEN
3000	COOPER SHELDON
3000	CUNEO LORAINE
3000	DETAMBLE MARTIN
3000	DETAMBLE VIRGINIA S
3000	DEWITT HERBERT S
3000	DEWITT RUTH T
3000	DOUGHERTY ROBERTA
3000	DURKIN DOROTHY
3000	ENZWEILER FLORA

3000	SLOAN LOUISE B
3000	SLOAN WILLIAM K
3000	SMILEY ELIZABETH J
3000	SMILEY THOMAS W
3000	STEVENS NANCY F
3000	STEVENS THOMAS L
3000	SWANSON ALDRIDGE B
3000	SWEENEY BERNARDINE
3000	TANZI GERTRUDE R
3000	TAYLOR JAMES R
3000	TINTHOFF ADELINE C
3000	UNKOVSKOY JOANNE C
3000	UNKOVSKOY SIMON
3000	VAN STRAATEN NATALIE
3000	VAN STRAATEN WILLIAM
3000	WESS WILLIAM WAYNE
3000	[illegible]
3000	WILK DOROTHY
3000	WITHERELL WILLIAM JR
3000	WOLL ALBERT E
3000	WOLL MARGUERITE H
3000	YORK MURIEL D
3000	ZIMMERMANN FRANCIS L
3000	ZIMMERMANN ROSEMARY
3000	MACHOL MARGOT E
3018	BEACOM MELISSA S
3018	BEACOM THOMAS HUMPHREY
3018	HORNING MICHAEL D
3018	KILEY FRANCIS T
3018	KILEY FRANK T
3018	KILEY VIRGINIA E
3018	MERLO JOHN
3018	MERLO MARIE A
3018	MERLO MERYLE S
3018	TOSCANO CHARLES S
3020	FRENCH ROBERT G
3020	JOHNSON VIRGIL C
3020	OBRIEN IRENE L
3020	SHRAGO DIANE M
3020	SHRAGO LAWRENCE A
3030	BROWN JAMES M
3030	CUNNINGHAM GLORIA
3030	ELMAN SOPHIE
3030	GHITZIS MIRIAM S
3030	GHITZIS MOISEY S
3030	HANSEN BERNICE
3030	HORZEMPA DOROTHY M
3030	IZENSTAT FLORENCE
3030	JACOBSON ROSE
3030	KARIL CHARLES E
3030	KESTEL KATHLEEN M
3030	LANZARATTA PHILIP A
3030	MARZEC FRANCES
3030	MINER RHODA L
3030	MINER SIDNEY
3030	NATHAN LEONARD
3030	RASMUSSEN DONALD L
3030	SCHROEDER MONICA
3030	SCHUIT MARTHA L
3030	VOGEL JOHN R
3030	WELSH JOHN P
3030	WELSH JOHN P
3030	WELSH SANDRA A
3030	WIEMUTH LOIS L

3033	LEFTWICH HAROLD A
3033	LEFTWICH JOYCE M
3033	LEON ARNOLD H
3033	LEON SALLY G
3033	LEVIN KENNETH S
3033	LEVIN MARCY L
3033	LEVINSON FAYE M
3033	LEVINSON JUNE B
3033	LEVITE EVELYN B
3033	LEVITE LEONARD D
3033	LORENZ KATHERINE M
3033	MARX ANITA
3033	MARX CHARLES L
3033	MARX RALPH J
3033	MAYER CLEMENCIA B
3033	MELL LAUREL H
3033	MILLER ETHEL R
3033	MILLER ROBERT D
3033	MILLER SUSAN M
3033	NASCA CATHERINE J
3033	NATHAN PHYLLIS R
3033	NEVETT THELMA L
3033	OPPENHEIMER GLADYS K
3033	OPPENHEIMER LAWRENCE G
3033	ORPHAN MARY G
3033	POLLOCK SUSAN F
3033	RAGO ANNE
3033	RAGO MARIE T
3033	ROBERTSON PAULA
3033	ROHDE BESSIE G
3033	ROSE ANDREA R
3033	ROZYCKI DOLORES L
3033	ROZYCKI JOANNA
3033	ROZYCKI SOPHIE A
3033	SALTIEL HELEN
3033	SCHNETTLER JAMES J
3033	SCHNETTLER SHIRLEY I
3033	SILBERMAN ALAN H
3033	SILBERMAN MARGARET
3033	SILVERSTEIN HERMAN
3033	SILVIUS GERTRUDE C
3033	SMITH HENRY
3033	SMITH IRENE
3033	SMITH JULIA R
3033	SMITH REED C
3033	STEVER EILEEN M
3033	STONESTREET WILLIAM L
3033	STUART DONNA G
3033	SUGARMAN BONNIE M
3033	THOMETZ CAROLYN B
3033	THOMETZ MICHAEL C
3033	TITUS FREDERICK L
3033	TITUS RUTH S
3033	ULASICH DIANE M
3033	ULASICH JUDITH M
3033	ULASICH SHARON R
3033	UMENHOFER ALMA E
3033	VIRNICK MILDRED
3033	WASHBURN ROBERTA L
3033	WEISS IDA
3033	WEISS LOIS M
3033	WHITE DOROTHY H
3033	WHITE VIRGIL H
3033	WOLF IDA H

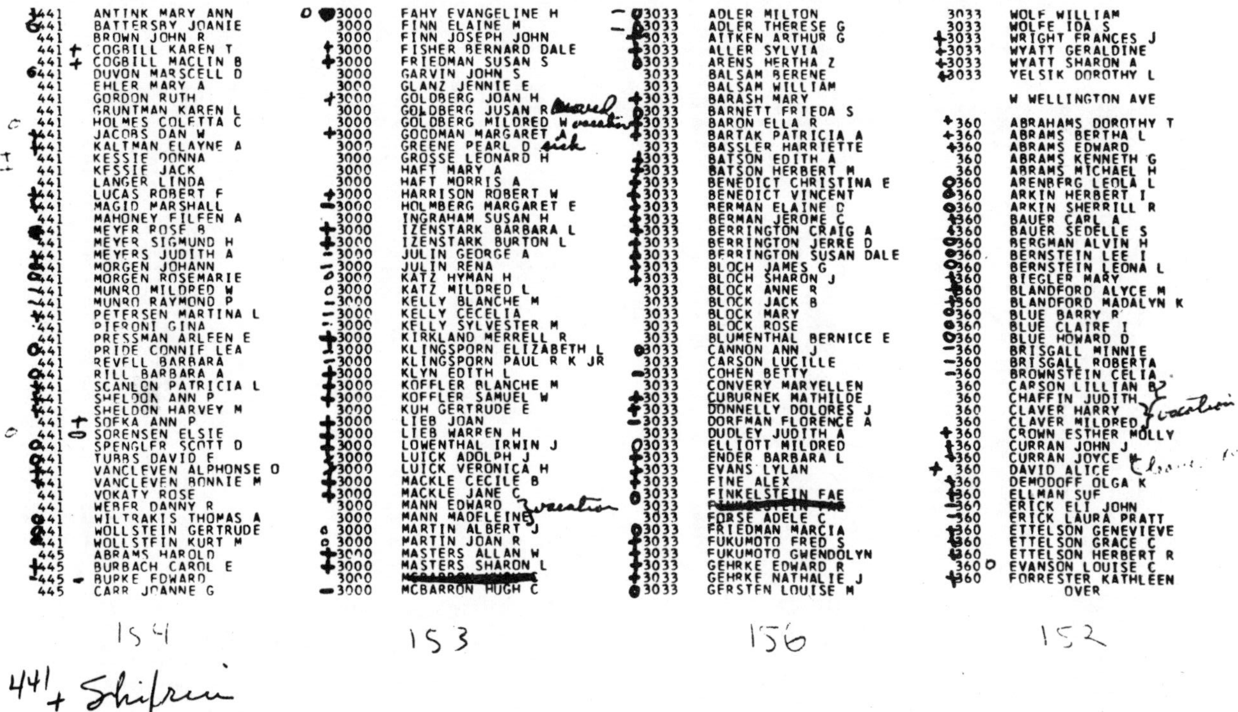

441	ANTINK MARY ANN
441	BATTERSBY JOANIE
441	BROWN JOHN R
441	COGBILL KAREN T
441	COGBILL MACLIN B
441	DUVON MARSCELL D
441	EHLER MARY A
441	GORDON RUTH
441	GRUNTMAN KAREN L
441	HOLMES COLETTA C
441	JACOBS DAN W
441	KALTMAN ELAYNE A
441	KESSIE DONNA
441	KESSIE JACK
441	LANGER LINDA
441	LUCAS ROBERT F
441	MAGID MARSHALL
441	MAHONEY EILEEN A
441	MEYER ROSE B
441	MEYER SIGMUND H
441	MEYERS JUDITH A
441	MORGEN JOHANN
441	MORGEN ROSEMARIE
441	MUNRO MILDRED W
441	MUNRO RAYMOND P
441	PETERSEN MARTINA L
441	PIERONI GINA
441	PRESSMAN ARLEEN E
441	PRIDE CONNIE LEA
441	REVELL BARBARA
441	RILL BARBARA A
441	SCANLON PATRICIA L
441	SHELDON ANN P
441	SHELDON HARVEY M
441	SOFKA ANN P
441	SORENSEN ELSIE
441	SPENGLER SCOTT D
441	TUBBS DAVID E
441	VANCLEVEN ALPHONSE O
441	VANCLEVEN BONNIE M
441	VOKATY ROSE
441	WEBER DANNY R
441	WILTRAKIS THOMAS A
441	WOLLSTEIN GERTRUDE
441	WOLLSTEIN KURT M
445	ABRAMS HAROLD
445	BURBACH CAROL E
445	BURKE EDWARD
445	CARR JOANNE G

3000	FAHY EVANGELINE H
3000	FINN ELAINE M
3000	FINN JOSEPH JOHN
3000	FISHER BERNARD DALE
3000	FRIEDMAN SUSAN S
3000	GARVIN JOHN S
3000	GLANZ JENNIE E
3000	GOLDBERG JOAN H
3000	GOLDBERG JUSAN R
3000	GOLDBERG MILDRED W
3000	GOODMAN MARGARET A
3000	GREENE PEARL D
3000	GROSSE LEONARD H
3000	HAFT MARY A
3000	HAFT MORRIS A
3000	HARRISON ROBERT W
3000	HOLMBERG MARGARET E
3000	INGRAHAM SUSAN H
3000	IZENSTARK BARBARA L
3000	IZENSTARK BURTON L
3000	JULIN GEORGE A
3000	JULIN RENA
3000	KATZ HYMAN H
3000	KATZ MILDRED L
3000	KELLY BLANCHE M
3000	KELLY CECELIA
3000	KELLY SYLVESTER M
3000	KIRKLAND MERRELL R
3000	KLINGSPORN ELIZABETH L
3000	KLINGSPORN PAUL R K JR
3000	KLYN EDITH L
3000	KOFFLER BLANCHE M
3000	KOFFLER SAMUEL W
3000	KUH GERTRUDE E
3000	LIEB JOAN
3000	LIEB WARREN H
3000	LOWENTHAL IRWIN J
3000	LUICK ADOLPH J
3000	LUICK VERONICA H
3000	MACKLE CECILE B
3000	MACKLE JANE C
3000	MANN EDWARD
3000	MANN MADELEINE
3000	MARTIN ALBERT J
3000	MARTIN JOAN R
3000	MASTERS ALLAN W
3000	MASTERS SHARON L
3000	[illegible]
3000	MCBARRON HUGH C

3033	ADLER MILTON
3033	ADLER THERESE G
3033	AITKEN ARTHUR G
3033	ALLER SYLVIA
3033	ARENS HERTHA Z
3033	BALSAM BERENE
3033	BALSAM WILLIAM
3033	BARASH MARY
3033	BARNETT FRIEDA S
3033	BARON ELLA R
3033	BARTAK PATRICIA A
3033	BASSLER HARRIETTE
3033	BATSON EDITH A
3033	BATSON HERBERT M
3033	BENEDICT CHRISTINA E
3033	BENEDICT VINCENT
3033	BERMAN ELAINE C
3033	BERMAN JEROME C
3033	BERRINGTON CRAIG A
3033	BERRINGTON JERRE D
3033	BERRINGTON SUSAN DALE
3033	BLOCH JAMES G
3033	BLOCH SHARON J
3033	BLOCK ANNE R
3033	BLOCK JACK B
3033	BLOCK MARY
3033	BLOCK ROSE
3033	BLUMENTHAL BERNICE E
3033	CANNON ANN J
3033	CARSON LUCILLE
3033	COHEN BETTY
3033	CONVERY MARYELLEN
3033	CUBURNEK MATHILDE
3033	DONNELLY DOLORES J
3033	DORFMAN FLORENCE A
3033	DUDLEY JUDITH A
3033	ELLIOTT MILDRED
3033	ENDER BARBARA L
3033	EVANS LYLAN
3033	FINE ALEX
3033	FINKELSTEIN FAE
3033	[illegible]
3033	FORSE ADELE C
3033	FRIEDMAN MARCIA
3033	FUKUMOTO FRED S
3033	FUKUMOTO GWENDOLYN
3033	GEHRKE EDWARD R
3033	GEHRKE NATHALIE J
3033	GERSTEN LOUISE M

3033	WOLF WILLIAM
3033	WOLFE IDA S
3033	WRIGHT FRANCES J
3033	WYATT GERALDINE
3033	WYATT SHARON A
3033	YELSIK DOROTHY L
	W WELLINGTON AVE
360	ABRAHAMS DOROTHY T
360	ABRAMS BERTHA L
360	ABRAMS EDWARD
360	ABRAMS KENNETH G
360	ABRAMS MICHAEL H
360	ARENBERG LEOLA L
360	ARKIN HERBERT I
360	ARKIN SHERRILL R
360	BAUER CARL A
360	BAUER SEDELLE S
360	BERGMAN ALVIN H
360	BERNSTEIN LEE I
360	BERNSTEIN LEONA L
360	BIEGLER MARY
360	BLANDFORD ALYCE M
360	BLANDFORD MADALYN K
360	BLUE BARRY R
360	BLUE CLAIRE I
360	BLUE HOWARD D
360	BRISGALL MINNIE
360	BRISGALL ROBERTA
360	BROWNSTEIN CELIA
360	CARSON LILLIAN B
360	CHAFFIN JUDITH
360	CLAVER HARRY
360	CLAVER MILDRED
360	CROWN ESTHER MOLLY
360	CURRAN JOHN J
360	CURRAN JOYCE M
360	DAVID ALICE
360	DEMODOFF OLGA K
360	ELLMAN SUE
360	ERICK ELI JOHN
360	ERICK LAURA PRATT
360	ETTELSON GENEVIEVE
360	ETTELSON GRACE C
360	ETTELSON HERBERT R
360	EVANSON LOUISE C
360	FORRESTER KATHLEEN

OVER

154 153 156 152

441 + Shifrin

W WELLINGTON AVE

360 GOETTLER EDWARD L
360 GOLDBERG ESTHER
360 GOLDBERG MINNA L
360 GOLDENBERG ESTHER
360 GOLDMAN DANIEL E
360 GOLDMAN MARGUERITE L
360 GOLDMAN MARIE
360 GOLDMAN WILLIAM B
360 GOLDSTONE JIMMIE E
360 GOODWIN LARUE
360 GORDON EDITH F
360 GROSSMAN FRANK
360 GROSSMAN HANNAH L
360 HARRIS BETTY H
360 HARRIS MELVYN J
360 HAUSER MARY K
360 HEILGENTHAL LORETTA M
360 HEIM JANIE
360 HEIM MICHAEL G
360 HELLMAN SARAH
360 HOPKINS JON F
360 HOPKINS MARILYN B
360 HYMAN RUTH S
360 HYMAN SOL H
360 ILIOPOULOS MILDRED A
360 JACOBSON FAY
360 JACOBSON ROSE
360 JANKOWSKI EDWARD
360 JANKOWSKI MARION A
360 KAPIL AJIT L
360 KAPIL DIANE G
360 KLEIN FRANCES R
360 KLEIN INEZ H
360 KLUTH MARY JO
360 KLUTH RAYMOND G
360 KNIGHT LILLIAN G P
360 LAMBERT MORTON N
360 LAMBERT SADYE H
360 LASER MEYER T
360 LAZAR IDA
360 LEAF ANNE B
360 LEAF MINNIE
360 LEAF RUTH
360 LIBMAN LAWRENCE H
360 LIBMAN NETTIE
360 LIPPITZ BLANCHE A
360 LIPPITZ MILTON C
360 MACCONO FRANCES D
360 MACCONO JOHN D
360 MARTIN JUDY R
360 MARTIN RIC
360 MULMAT JACK
360 MULMAT STELLA
360 OBRIEN ROSEMARY I
360 PECK RICHARD
360 PRICE JANET
360 PRIESS BEATRICE L
360 PRIESS HAROLD L
360 QUINLAN WILLIAM R
360 RAY CHARLOTTE
360 RAY HERMAN
360 REDEL BLANCHE G
360 ROSENBLOOM JAMES L
360 ROSENBLOOM JANE A
360 ROTFELD LOUIS
360 ROTFELD MARJORIE
360 SADEV LEON
360 SADEV LILLIAN
360 SAMBURS MARION R
360 SAMBURS NATHAN C
360 SANDEL EDWIN
360 SANDEL ROSE
360 SCHNEIDER IRVING J
360 SCHNEIDER REVA P
360 SCHOR CASEY
360 SCHOR RUTH
360 SILVERMAN BEA
360 SILVERMAN MARILY
360 SILVERMAN MOLLIE
360 SLOAN ESTHER F
360 SMELTZER JOHN A
360 SMITH ROBERT H
360 SOLOTROFF DOROTHY H
360 SOLOTROFF LOUIS
360 SPIELBERG ANNE
360 SPIELBERG S WALTER
360 STEIDEN ELIZABETH L
360 STONE ANNA R
360 STONE IRVING C
360 STONE JACK I
360 STRATTON LIOTA C
360 TECOTZKY MAX
360 WALZER FRIEDA L
360 WEINBERG FAYE
360 WEINBERG JERRY
360 WEINBERG MURIEL K
360 WOISLAW LINDA L
360 WOISLAW WILLIAM A
360 WONNBERGER MARJORIE R
360 WONNBERGER PAUL H
360 ZUCKERBERG FANNIE
404 VOSE HAMILTON III
404 VOSE LUCINDA M
406 BROWN RALPH E
406 BROWN SUZANNE W
410 ELLBOGEN JEANNE M
410 ELLBOGEN RICHARD S
410 ELLBOGEN STEVE S JR
412 FRIEDMAN ELMER A
412 FRIEDMAN SHIRLEY S
412 STERN ESTHER M
412 STERN MICHAEL E
414 GINGISS CARMEL A
416 COLSON GORDON F
416 COLSON HAZEL HORNER
418 ROCKWELL DOROTHY J
418 ROCKWELL DUDLEY N
420 ABBOTT ANITA
420 ABBOTT ARTHUR
420 ABBOTT MARGARET E
422 PORTER LAURA RAYNAIR
422 PORTER LOUIS P JR
424 1/2 BULGER JOHN B
424 1/2 BULGER MARY JANE
424 KAUFMAN ARNOLD M
424 KAUFMAN HELEN S
426 FERRIS CHARLES J
426 RHEINSTROM CELENE
426 RHEINSTROM MEYER I
426 RHEINSTROM RICHARD A
426 RHEINSTROM STEPHEN D
428 CARLETON DIANA S
428 CARLETON ROBERT F
428 MAREMONT ANDREA F
428 MAREMONT JAMES K
432 AMBOS GLORIA M
432 BUCKLEY THOMAS J
432 COOPER ALLEN R
432 CROOK MICHAEL R
432 ERICKSON JOHN W
432 FRANKLIN DONALD B
432 FRANKLIN JOYCE H
432 KELLY JOHN H
432 LAFFEY MARY T
432 NESBITT MARY F
432 NESBITT RUSSELL U
432 PYLE MARY E
432 SATTELMAIER ERWIN J
432 SMITH CHERRY F
432 TERRY BOB K
432 TERRY JACQUELINE
432 TRAUB BARBARA A
432 VINOKUROFF JEAN
432 WALSH MICHAEL T
432 WEISS FLORICE D
434 ARMSTRONG CATHERINE D
434 BRECKENRIDGE DONALD J
434 BRECKENRIDGE HELEN K
434 BRENNER H BLISS
434 CHAPIN SUSAN A
434 COHN LIZBETH J
434 CONNAUGHTON DENNIS M
434 CUNNANE MARGARET JOAN
434 EHRMANN FRANK
434 FOGEL RUTH
434 GOULART CHRISTINA F
434 GOULART EDWIN A
434 GRADY WILLIAM G
434 GRONOW MABEL F
434 HEIDENTHAL ROBERTA A
434 HELMBOLDT JANE S
434 HENDERICKSON ARMAS
434 HENDERICKSON LEMPI
434 HOLLENDER MILDRED
434 LAZARUS HENRY L
434 LEE GERALD
434 LEVY DAVID
434 LEVY SARAH H
434 MAATF MARGARET
434 MATZ CAROL
434 MCGINNES ELISABETH H
434 MESSMER PATRICIA A
434 MESSMER PATRICIA ANN
434 MILLER LAWRANCE J
434 MILLER LAWRENCE T
434 MOY MARK G
434 MUELLER EDNA C
434 OSULLIVAN BARBARA M
434 PAISLEY JAMES C
434 PATRICK LINDA M
434 PATRICK LINDA M
434 PIERSON LINDA L
434 PINSKY SHARON F
434 POPA MARY
434 POW LAURA M
434 PRAIRIE SANDRA F
434 QUIGLEY SUSAN M
434 REINKE DONALD W
434 REYNOLDS JOHN H
434 ROSENTHAL ANNE
434 ROSSIE ALBERT B
434 SAVITT STEPHEN R
434 SCHNELL CARDINAL L
434 SIEGEL ADRIENNE G
434 SIEKERSKI CLIFFORD P
434 SIMMONDS SUSAN C
434 SMITH ALBERTA M
434 STRAUSS BARBARA
434 STRONG LYDIA C
434 TEMPLE PAIGE
434 ULRICH KENNETH G
434 WYERS MARTHA M
442 BECKER ALLEN
442 BECKER DEBRAH A
442 FRANKEL RUTH H
442 GLINK RONALD M
442 GLINK SUSANNE K
442 GOEEN ETHEL C
442 GOEEN WILLIAM H
442 GOLDBERG HARVEY S
442 GOLDBERG JOANN C
442 GOLDBERG MARCIA ANNE
442 HABER DOROTHY R
442 HABER SAMUEL S
442 HOLLER DORIS B
442 HOLLER GORDON P
442 HOLLER MARSHALL M
442 HOLLER PAUL D
442 KESTNBAUM KATE T
442 KESTNBAUM ROBERT D
442 KOFF MIRIAM W
442 KOFF ROBERT H
442 KURTZON KENNETH C
442 KURTZON MICHAEL STEVEN
442 KURTZON SHIRLEY
442 LERNER LOUIS A
442 LERNER SUSAN
442 MANILOW LORETTA
442 MARIENTHAL GEORGE E
442 MARIENTHAL JEANNE P
442 MINER CHARLOTTE W
442 MINER MARVIN
442 NISSMAN GRACE
442 NISSMAN MORRIS
442 SCHULTZ CHESTER H
442 SCHULTZ CORINNE G
442 SHELL HELEN N
442 SHELL IRVING W
442 SIMS RUTH V
442 SWARTCHILD BEATRICE
442 SWARTCHILD WILLIAM JR
442 TINSLEY ABBY GRACE
442 TINSLEY MILTON
442 TINSLEY PHYLLIS S
442 TULSKY ALEX S DR
442 TULSKY KLARA G
442 WOLBACH MARY L
442 WOLBACH MURRAY JR
442 WOLBACH MURRAY III
442 ZOUB BARBARA H

The undersigned members of the Board of Election Commissioners of the City of Chicago certify that the names on the list are the names of all voters entitled to vote at the February 23, 1971 Municipal Primary and Aldermanic Elections in the Precinct indicated on the top hereof and, according to the Election Code this list is prima facie evidence that the electors whose names appear hereon are entitled to vote. This list is subject to corrections and revisions that may be published in a supplemental list subsequent hereto.

Chicago, January, 1971

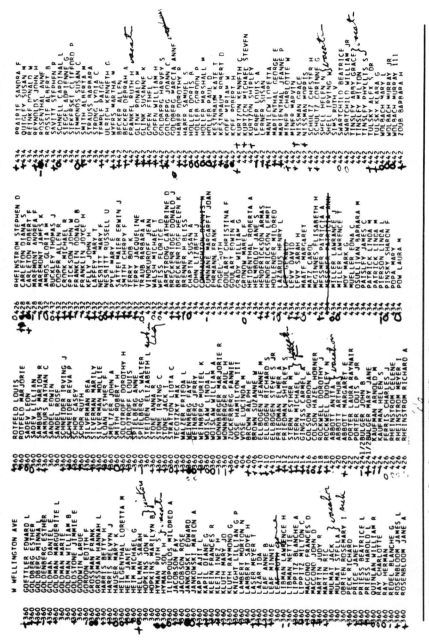

> and this is getting our plus vote out. And this is the whole point of what this really important canvass is about — locating Bernie's favorable vote and at the same time educating people to him in the process of getting their favorable response.[32]

Each worker develops his own way of talking with voters. Generally, however, you will want to organize your presentation around the following points:

1. Introduce yourself. ("I'm Joe Smith, a volunteer working to elect Independent Bernard Weisberg as a delegate to the Constitutional Convention.")
2. Hand the voter a piece of campaign literature and tell your candidate's virtues in two or three sentences.
3. Ask if you may count on the voter's support for your candidate.
4. Thank the voter and leave as quickly and courteously as possible.

The entire discussion with a voter should take only five minutes. If there are one hundred families in your precinct, a canvass of every family can be completed in something less than ten hours. With three workers in the precinct, each will have to work only slightly over three hours. That is, you can finish the job *if you:*

1. *Don't engage in long discussions.* If the voter has numerous detailed questions, have him call headquarters for the answers. You have hundreds of voters to see. In the hour you spend talking to a single voter you could have canvassed twenty others.
2. *Don't engage in arguments.* You may think you have won the argument, but your candidate has lost a vote and those of all the voters you won't have time to see.
3. *Do start early.* Don't put off the job for weeks, but begin as soon as you have received canvassing instructions and materials.
4. *Do work systematically.* Divide the list of voters to be seen among the workers available to do the job, and divide your list so that you canvass a portion of the voters each week.

5. *Do recruit new workers to help.* As you go to each home, watch for potential workers. They are even more valuable than plus voters. If you find citizens interested in the campaign, encourage them to work along with you. After you have recruited more than two or three co-workers, turn in the other names of potential workers to headquarters so that they can be employed in covering some of the uncovered precincts. In sharing your workers remember that the point of the campaign is to win the election, not simply to carry your precinct.

Accuracy is crucial in a good canvass. To achieve accuracy, workers must understand the +, –, and 0 symbols they mark on the poll lists and the reason for them. On election day you will work very hard to get every one of your *plus voters* to vote. You will completely ignore the *minus voters.* Unless there are special considerations like ethnic identification with the candidate or strong support for your candidate in the rest of the precinct, you will also ignore *zero voters.* In short, you will be working from 5 A.M. to 6 P.M. to insure that every one of the voters known to be favorable to your candidate votes. Obviously, to do this job effectively you must know which voters are favorable to your candidate. That is the reason for the canvass. Workers must be careful in their evaluations of the voters. Voters who can be counted on to vote for your candidate, not voters who smile in a friendly manner when talking to you, are the ones to be identified with a plus. Score as plus voters only those who answer *Yes* to the question "May we count on your support?"

Given the importance of this task, you may well be wondering why it is left to the last three or four weeks before the election. There are three reasons. First, the registration drive immediately precedes the canvass and the two can not be done simultaneously. Second, precinct workers work best within definite time periods rather than at their leisure over several months. If there is not a limited time and a specific job to be done, most workers will keep putting the work off. Finally, most voters don't have enough information about the candidates and the elections to make their choice until close to election day. It is only in this period that media coverage is very great or voter interest very high. Asking for whom voters plan to vote much earlier is a waste of time. As with the registration campaign, you will have less than a month to complete the canvass and reports of your progress will be requested each week.

In conclusion, the canvass is the most crucial phase of the campaign. If it is done well, your chances of winning are very good. If workers fail to contact enough voters or fail to discern their preferences or fail to be good representatives of your candidate, then there will not be the favorable *plus voters* to run to the polls on election day and all is lost. No candidate wins on good looks or publicity or good stands on the issues alone. To win the election campaign workers contact voters personally, ask for their vote, and remind them of their duty on election day. The other side will be working too, but they can be beaten if enough volunteers are willing to put in the time and if they work systematically and effectively. Particularly over a period of several campaigns, dramatic results can be achieved by good precinct work. This is exemplified by the transformation of three precincts in Chicago's 44th Ward as shown in Table 4. The voters in these precincts, which went as much as four to one for the Regular Democrats in 1968, were almost evenly divided by the aldermanic primary in 1969, and voted heavily in favor of Weisberg (four to one in Precinct 11) by 1970. This is an example of political change at grass roots. When multiplied by all the precincts in Chicago's 9th Congressional District which have changed since 1968, it becomes obvious that the north side of Chicago has been freed from the automatic and total machine domination which has lasted for more than one hundred years. This change was brought about through door-to-door precinct work for good candidates.

While the door-to-door effort is going on in the precincts, the candidate is not idle. Continuing the existing schedule of three or four coffees a day to induce more citizens to become campaign volunteers, a luncheon to raise money, a press conference to get publicity, and staff meetings to develop campaign strategy, the candidate adds to his activities meeting voters at bus stops each morning from 7:00 to 9:00 A.M., shopping center appearances every weekend, and walking tours of precincts in the afternoons. By talking with voters at bus stops, at

Table 4

Election Results In Selected 44th Ward Precincts

Precinct No.	1968 McCARTHY CAMPAIGN Independent (Montgomery)	Reg. Dem. (Dunne)	1969 ALDERMANIC CAMPAIGN Independent (Singer)	Reg. Dem. (Gaughan)	Republican (White)	Other (Rosenblum)
2	23	115	110	121	72	4
10	57	73	71	79	71	3
11	21	36	127	38	122	5

Precinct No.	1970 CONSTITUTIONAL CONVENTION CAMPAIGN* Independent (Weisberg)	Reg. Dem. (Hennigan)	Reg. Dem. (Tuchow)	Republican (Harvey)
2	215	163	90	112
10	110	80	96	98
11	164	42	34	163

*Note: Each voter could cast two votes in the election. Thus, many Weisberg supporters voted for Bennett Harvey as well and many Democrats voted for both Democratic candidates.

stores, and in their homes, the candidate demonstrates his interest in their problems and makes the job of the precinct worker much easier. The word will quickly get around that the candidate personally visited the area, something previous candidates who could rely upon the party machine never bothered to do.

Ghetto campaigns

So far this handbook has treated all campaigns as if they were the same. Certain general principles do apply in every case: workers must contact voters, record voter preferences, and get favorable voters to the polls on election day. However, ghetto campaigns have special problems in accomplishing these tasks. They suffer from two liabilities: 1) lack of resources such as volunteer workers, trained staff, and money, and 2) special difficulties in convincing voters to support independent candidates or even ascertaining their preferences.

Ghetto campaigns are critical to our efforts for political change. These communities are the ones most likely to suffer from political oppression and to benefit most from new political leadership. They are the ones in the greatest need of the community control made possible by participatory politics. Finally, they are the great strongholds by which the Democratic Party machine controls the major cities of America. They give eighty or ninety percent of their votes to support candidates who do not serve, but control them through payoffs and fear. In the long run, if participatory politics is to become a national political force, it must exist in ghettos as well as middle class communities.

The problem of inadequate resources for ghetto campaigns requires a dual solution. First, more resources — particularly skilled manpower — must be raised within the ghetto itself. The situation can be remedied to some extent by participatory campaigns outside of the ghetto employing people from the ghetto on campaign staffs. It can be better solved by running strong ghetto campaigns. It may take one campaign for a candidate to become known, for people to trust him, and to let campaign workers and staff have the experience necessary to win the second time around. However, even with trained campaign leaders, money remains a scarce resource, and this must, in part, be provided by the middle class community. In the 1969 aldermanic campaign John Stevens spent three thousand dollars to run in Chicago's racially mixed 42nd ward. He came within 743 votes of forcing a run-off with the Regular Democratic candidate. A few dollars more and a few more workers — white or black — and that election could have been won. Citizens from middle-class communities must be willing to help subsidize such campaigns. In Chicago one means of doing this is through a group called the Committee for an Effective City Council which raises money and funnels donations to selected aldermanic races in both ghetto and middle-class wards where independents have some prospect of victory. Whatever the mechanism, means must be found to channel money from outside into ghetto campaigns. Most money will still have to be raised internally by the campaign, but a thousand dollars of outside support can mean a lot for campaign morale and for hiring adequate staff, opening headquarters, and printing necessary campaign literature.

Fund raising within the ghetto itself differs considerably from that in middle class communities. First of all, facilities and services are more likely to be raised from institutions such as churches, while these often play a more neutral, non-partisan role in non-ghetto areas. Thus, the John Stevens campaign in 1969 was run first from a church community center and, after that mysteriously burned down, from the basement of St. Dominic's Church. However, fund-raising events in both the ghetto and middle-class communities are needed. Many of the small donations are raised from dances thrown by teenagers. Added to these are outside contributions from groups like the Committee for an Effective City Council or from parties in the middle class sections of the ward. Ghetto campaigns thus cost less because facilities and services are donated more frequently, but the shoestring budget raised from events such as dances in the poor areas and coffees in the rich areas falls short of what is really needed. In 1971 when John Stevens ran a second time, his three thousand dollar budget was increased to nine thousand dollars, but that was still short of the fifteen to twenty thousand dollars needed for a first-class campaign.

He was defeated a second time.

The other problem in ghetto campaigns — obtaining honest responses from the residents — is not so easily resolved. Since many ghetto dwellers live at a bare subsistence level and are dependent upon various forms of public assistance, they are often at the mercy (or believe themselves to be at the mercy) of regular party precinct captains. He may be able to terminate their welfare payments, have them thrown out of public housing, or have them fired from government jobs.

Thus, for a variety of reasons, ghetto dwellers will tend to support regular party candidates. But what is worse, most of them won't tell canvassers the truth about how they plan to vote. They will "jive" you. After all, why should they make an enemy when they can just say they will vote for your candidate? Especially if you are supporting a Black candidate in a Black ward against a white opponent, most citizens will tell you they are going to vote for your candidate even though they know all along that they will vote for the regular party's candidate instead.

Thus, canvassers return with 400 plus voters on their poll lists and no zeroes, no minuses. That means that these precincts cannot be effectively worked on election day. You cannot make the effort to get all voters to the polls on election day, both because the task is too much to accomplish in a single day and because too many of the voters will vote against your candidate. In electoral campaigns you need to be able to identify accurately your own supporters and concentrate on getting them to vote. The only remedy for the tendency of ghetto voters to jive volunteers is well-trained precinct workers who carefully probe the voter's initial response to be sure that most of those he marks with a plus on the poll list will really vote for his candidate on election day.

Because of the shortage of precinct workers in most ghetto campaigns — particularly a shortage of indigenous workers — there is a great temptation to *hire* high school students or people who say they have worked in previous campaigns. Usually these folks will take your money, but bring you no votes. It is much safer to hire only members of the central campaign staff or pay workers only for the time taken from their regular job to work on election day. Participatory politics depends primarily on people being willing to participate voluntarily in the electoral process. Highly-paid, mercenary armies of workers are simply no substitute. Besides, the political machine undoubtably pays better wages than you can offer.

All these factors make canvassing in ghetto campaigns very difficult. (In the next chapter some attention will be paid to vote fraud which is also a major problem in the ghettos.) But despite these problems, favorable voters must be located and brought to the polls. Sound trucks, posters, campaign literature, public relations, and just talking to the voters won't win elections. An effective voter canvass will — even in the most difficult political situations. As we get more experience in running participatory campaigns in ghetto communities, special techniques will undoubtedly be refined and adapted. Then instead of the general descriptions of campaigns like those in Carmichael and Hamilton's *Black Power,* someone may write a special handbook for participatory politics in America's ghettos.[33]

Canvassing high rises

At the opposite end of the socio-economic spectrum a different set of problems exists. Upper middle class and wealthy citizens in major cities often live in large, high-rise apartments. In Chicago some of these mammoth buildings contain over a thousand voters and, thus, cannot be ignored. Yet, their residents are surprisingly isolated. Seldom do they know their neighbors on the same floor, much less in other parts of the building or in the community outside their protective walls. Their privacy is zealously protected by watchful doormen and apartment managers.

The first problem for a participatory campaign is to find workers in these buildings. One solution is to hold coffees at which the residents can meet the candidate. But if you do not have workers in the building, sponsoring such a coffee may be difficult. In such cases, an area chairman or coffee coordinator must first call contacts or friends of other campaign workers or simply the list of registered voters until a willing hostess can be found. Then all residents must receive a coffee invitation and be personally invited to attend. After all these efforts, attendance may still be very disappointing. But, hopefully, enough indigenous workers can be signed up to work at least their own building.

In an inner-city district with more than a hundred high rise apartments, successful coffees will not be possible at all of them. The remaining buildings will have to be worked by outside volunteers. The difficulty is getting into the building to canvass. Other than living in the building, there are four practical methods of gaining entrance:[34] 1) to have a contact who lives in the building let you in, 2) to walk in at the same time as someone who lives in the building and has a key, 3) to call people listed on the precinct poll list over the speaker system until you find someone willing to talk about the election to let you in, and 4) if there is a doorman, to walk up, say hello and act as if you expect him to open the door for you — often he will. If none of these work, ask the manager for admittance or, at least, permission to place campaign literature in the mailboxes.

After trying every trick, you may get in the building only to find irate residents calling the manager to have you thrown out. Three tactics remain to be tried. You can put five or more workers in the building to canvass different floors simultaneously. By the time the management throws them all out, the bulk of the building will have been canvassed.

If a door-to-door canvass is impossible because of an inability to get in or because of a lack of willing workers, do a telephone canvass. The results are less desirable but far superior to no canvass at all. A successful telephone canvass is preceded by leafletting or mailing campaign brochures to each resident. Then the telephone numbers for each registered voter in the precinct are found in a reverse telephone directory where telephone numbers are listed by address. As in the door-to-door canvass, the campaign worker introduces himself to the person he calls, gives a brief statement of the candidate's virtues, finds out the voter's preference, and marks the poll list.

In phone canvassing, as in face-to-face canvassing, the

> critical element is the kind and quality of interaction between you and each voter. You will be in effect John Kearney's personal representative. Most voters will vote for John if they feel that you are trustworthy and reasonably well informed. You have to sell yourself in order to sell John. Your own good judgment, politeness and helpfulness are worth more than any qualities that John has.
>
> In this regard, relying on a standard spiel type of approach is probably the single most self-defeating thing you can do. It makes you seem insincere and uncaring, as if you were only going through the motions of canvassing. Your most difficult job will be to maintain your own authenticity, to continue to be yourself — time after time, call after call. Your own genuineness and spontaneity — whether quick and enthusiastic, serious or bashful — are your strongest assets.[35]

If you lack the manpower for a telephone canvass, only a mailing or blitz can be made. Blitz results were reported in Chapter III and the results of a mailing are shown in Table 5. In the 1968 campaign to elect McCarthy delegates in the 9th Congressional District of Illinois, a mailing consisting of a letter and campaign flyer was sent to six high-rise precincts which were otherwise uncovered. Unfortunately these precincts turned out to be heavily Republican-oriented, and most voters could not be persuaded to vote in the Democratic primary. The results were not worth the cost of the mailing in that campaign. In the two precincts in which there were from 150 to 200 voters who voted Democratic, the percentage going to McCarthy delegates was 9-14%. For all six precincts only twenty-two percent of the vote went for McCarthy delegates and in no precinct were more than 31 votes received. Of 2500 voters who received these letters, less than four percent voted for the independent delegates. These results are so poor that it would have been better if nothing at all had been done — and it would have been $200 cheaper.

Table 5

Vote in Chicago's 42nd Ward High-rise Precincts Which Received Information by Mail During the Democratic Primary Election, 1968

	McCarthy Delegate (Montgomery)		Regular Dem. Delegate (Dunne)	
Precinct No.	No. Votes	Percent of Dem. Vote	No. Votes	Percent of Dem. Vote
20	14	(9%)	136	(91%)
25	3	(18%)	14	(82%)
26	12	(31%)	27	(69%)
27	18	(44%)	23	(56%)
49	31	(14%)	188	(86%)
55	14	(26%)	40	(74%)
TOTAL	92	(22%)	428	(78%)

The results may well be quite different when, as in Winthrop Rockefeller's 1968 campaign for reelection as governor of Arkansas, individually computer-composed and typewritten letters can be sent to 200,000 voters. But for a small participatory campaign, mass mailings are very costly. However, individualized letters from community leaders to their social clubs, church groups, and neighbors may be effective and have been used in the Singer and Weisberg campaigns to good effect. Moreover, in my own campaign, letters of endorsement like the ones shown on pages 129, 130, did prove useful in identifying me with a political tradition of honest, independent officials representing our community. Such letters did serve to prepare voters to be receptive when called on by precinct workers. The first letter was written by three previously-elected independents and mailed to the entire district. The second, written by Alderman Singer, was sent only to his former constituents, particularly to those in the more conservative areas of the ward. The letter from Latin leaders was mailed to everyone with Spanish surnames. Such letters by themselves can only introduce your candidate to the voter. It still takes precinct worker follow-up to win an election.

Rural campaigns

Rural campaigns differ in several particulars from those run in either cities or suburbs, but the intent is the same — to personally contact the voters. The primary differences between urban and rural campaigns are 1) money, 2) tools for campaigning and 3) distances. Thus, James Kessler reports spending less than $3,000 in a successful primary battle to become the Republican candidate for state senate in a rural district in Indiana in 1963. Half of the funds were his own and half were raised from some thirty-eight contributors.[36] Much more money would be needed to finance a contested race in a major city.

The easily available campaign tools and political information in urban districts may be completely lacking in rural areas. Thus, the first task of the campaign may be to develop a list of registered voters, to determine their party affiliation from assorted public and private records, to find precinct maps and canvassing routes, and to put together the necessary kits of registration information and campaign literature. All of this must be done before either registration drives or the voter canvass can be launched.

Greater distances involved in rural canvassing require more automobiles and create transportation problems not faced in urban districts. It also takes longer to canvass the voters. Much coordination and planning is required in scheduling and holding meetings in the larger districts and getting the candidate to all parts of the district. Time becomes a scarce commodity just because it takes canvassers, candidate, and all campaign personnel so long to traverse the district.

Recruiting sufficient volunteers to canvass rural areas can be something of a problem unless there happen to be colleges within the district. Volunteer canvassers seem to produce good results in spite

Citizens for Simpson.

CAMPAIGN CHAIRMAN
Bernard Weisberg
HONORARY CHAIRMEN
Alderman Bill Singer
Representative Bruce Douglas

HEADQUARTERS
1045 West Belmont
Chicago, Illinois 60657
Phone 525-6034

January, 1971

<u>A MESSAGE TO OUR FRIENDS IN THE LAKEVIEW AREA</u>

First, we would like to extend a collective "thank you" for your support in the past two years. We have tried to bring a new and responsible form of government-by-the-citizens to the community.

Your participation and interest in the vital issues of state, city and community helped bring us to public office. But more importantly it reflected a concern for important matters affecting all our lives. The success of the new Illinois Constitution and of the Judicial Merit Selection proposition in this community indicates a concern for issues - not simply personalities - and with good government instead of "politics as usual."

Now we want to call your attention to a new campaign and an outstanding candidate for public office.

At the request of many people in the community, <u>Dick Simpson is running for Alderman of the new 44th Ward</u>.

Dick is an outstanding teacher at the University of Illinois Circle Campus, an award-winning film-maker and author in the field of political science. But he is more than just a scholar, <u>he is a man who gets things done</u>.

Dick founded the Independent Precinct Organization, which brought genuine citizen participation in politics to the North Side. We know him as both friend and mentor, for without him, we believe, little that has been accomplished in the community would have been possible.

We are especially pleased that he agreed to run for this important office, and we know he will perform ably and well. We are proud that he asked us to assume roles in his campaign - <u>and we strongly urge you to support him at the polls on February 23rd</u>.

Very sincerely,

William S. Singer — Bernard Weisberg — Dr. Bruce Douglas

P.S. Dick needs your active help. His headquarters is located at 1045 W. Belmont - or call 525-6034

William S. Singer
Alderman, 44th Ward

Bernard Weisberg
Delegate to the Illinois Constitutional Convention

Dr. Bruce Douglas
State Representative (D-11)

Dick Simpson
44th Ward
Aldermanic Candidate

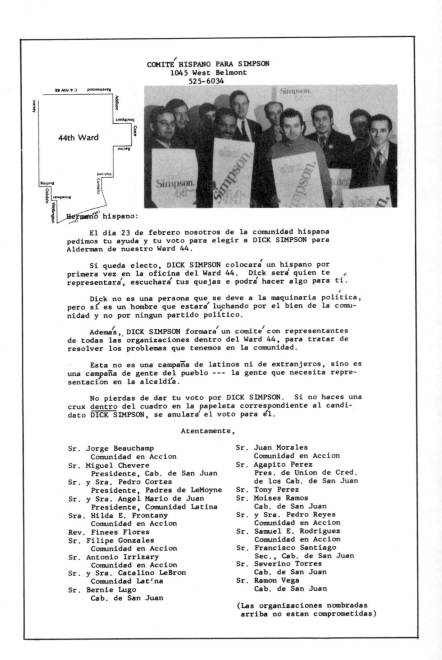

COMITÉ HISPANO PARA SIMPSON
1045 West Belmont
525-6034

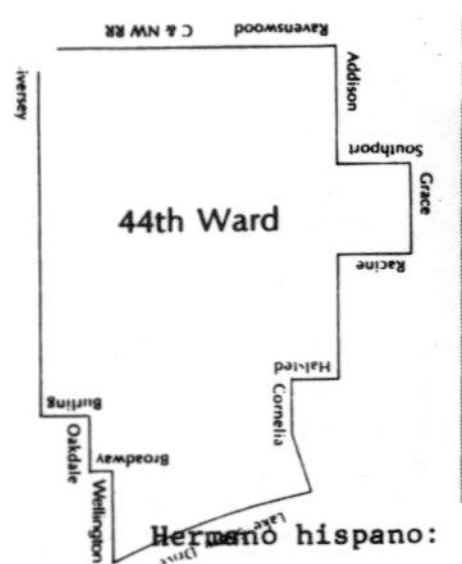

Hermano hispano:

El dia 23 de febrero nosotros de la comunidad hispana pedimos tu ayuda y tu voto para elegir a DICK SIMPSON para Alderman de nuestro Ward 44.

Si queda electo, DICK SIMPSON colocará un hispano por primera vez en la oficina del Ward 44. Dick será quien te representará, escuchará tus quejas e podrá hacer algo para tí.

Dick no es una persona que se deve a la maquinaria política, pero sí es un hombre que estará luchando por el bien de la comunidad y no por ningun partido político.

Además, DICK SIMPSON formará un comité con representantes de todas las organizaciones dentro del Ward 44, para tratar de resolver los problemas que tenemos en la comunidad.

Esta no es una campaña de latinos ni de extranjeros, sino es una campaña de gente del pueblo --- la gente que necesita representación en la alcaldía.

No pierdas de dar tu voto por DICK SIMPSON. Si no haces una crux dentro del cuadro en la papeleta correspondiente al candidato DICK SIMPSON, se anulará el voto para él.

Atentamente,

Sr. Jorge Beauchamp
Comunidad en Accion
Sr. Miguel Chevere
Presidente, Cab. de San Juan
Sr. y Sra. Pedro Cortes
Presidente, Padres de LeMoyne
Sr. y Sra. Angel Mario de Juan
Presidente, Comunidad Latina
Sra. Hilda E. Frontany
Comunidad en Accion
Rev. Finees Flores
Sr. Filipe Gonzales
Comunidad en Accion
Sr. Antonio Irrizary
Comunidad en Accion
Sr. y Sra. Catalino LeBron
Comunidad Latina
Sr. Bernie Lugo
Cab. de San Juan

Sr. Juan Morales
Comunidad en Accion
Sr. Agapito Perez
Pres. de Union de Cred. de los Cab. de San Juan
Sr. Tony Perez
Sr. Moises Ramos
Cab. de San Juan
Sr. y Sra. Pedro Reyes
Comunidad en Accion
Sr. Samuel E. Rodriguez
Comunidad en Accion
Sr. Francisco Santiago
Sec., Cab. de San Juan
Sr. Severino Torres
Cab. de San Juan
Sr. Ramon Vega
Cab. de San Juan

(Las organizaciones nombradas arriba no estan comprometidas)

of the legendary rural distrust of outsiders. The parties also tend to be weak in rural districts and to hold voters by primeval rather than modern ties.

In Bloomington, Indiana, McCarthy Democrats were able to win contested races for precinct committeeman simply by canvassing all the voters. Many rural voters, just like urban voters, have never been visited by a campaign worker before. Their votes are available almost for the asking.

Problems of a participatory campaign

Participatory politics is not a particularly easy, even if it is an honorable way, to power. Successful campaigns can be waged, but they should not be entered blindly. You should know what you are getting into and be willing to sacrifice the work, the time, and the money to win. In a letter to the editor of a local Chicago paper, a candidate who had entered and lost three separate elections offered the following warning:

> I would not encourage anyone to challenge through the electoral process without serious consideration of the following realities:
>
> The first is the difficulty of staffing a campaign. There are very few good political organizers in the state, and these few are snapped up by the 'glamour' campaigns. There also is a relatively small number of experienced volunteers. A core of experienced volunteers is essential to train others . . .
>
> The second is finances. Any such campaign takes all a candidate has or all he can borrow. He must be prepared to sacrifice everything, for political campaigns are extremely expensive. Indeed, political campaigns would be absolutely impossible except for persons of wealth, if it

were not for those [other citizens] willing to contribute.

The third is the diminuation of the candidate's personal effectiveness as a result of his candidacy . . . . I have met people who have been told by their Democratic precinct workers that I was one or more of the following: a Communist, a Republican, a drunk, a sex maniac, a pervert. There are probably many others that I have yet to hear of.

The fourth is the difficulty of presenting oneself through the news media. Regular organization candidates are accepted on face value. Insurgents must always prove themselves first and even then are given little space.

The fifth is the fact that even if an insurgent gets his voters to the polls, in many cases their votes will not be fairly cast and counted. The adversary process of elections recognizes only Democrats and Republicans. The insurgent has no one to speak for him . . . .

The sixth is the fact that anything that happens to an insurgent's workers during a campaign in a poor area is interpreted by other supporters and voters as a malevolent act on the part of the regular organization and causes real fear . . . .

The seventh is the fact that those who run well and lose often become unemployable in Chicago, except through the organization that beats them . . . .

Despite all of this, the good man who will still tilt against the windmills is deserving of any help I can give him and, I would hope, many others in the community as well.[37]

Participatory politics, which may hold the potential of reforming all of American politics, requires two qualities of its participants: courage and the dedication to run a skillful and effective campaign. The work is hard, the sacrifices demanded of both the candidate and the workers are many, but each victory, each step on the road of political reform makes all the work and all the sacrifices worthwhile.

Questions

1. What are the purposes of the canvass and how do the use of plus, minus and zero symbols help to accomplish that purpose? pp. 109, 113, 117-118

2. Why is it so difficult in a ghetto campaign to raise money and to get an accurate plus list? What effect does that have on campaigning? pp. 122-123

3. How can the problem of gaining access to wealthy high-rise buildings be overcome? pp. 124-126

4. What are the differences between urban and rural campaigns? What changes would have to be made in the techniques suggested in this handbook to adapt them to rural campaigning? pp.128-131

5. What are some of the campaign realities which an independent candidate for public office must face? Given these difficulties, why are people willing to run for office and work in participatory campaigns? pp. 131-333

Workshop Exercise

An understanding of door-to-door canvassing can be gained to a certain extent by role-playing in small groups. In each of the following situations have one member of the group play the role of the canvasser for an independent candidate and the other the role of the voter:

1. Precinct worker and staunch Republican male voter

2. Precinct worker and Democratic housewife
3. Precinct worker and uncertain independent voter
4. Precinct worker and "little old lady"
5. Precinct worker and a "radical"

After each scene, members of the group should criticize the job done by the precinct worker — watching particularly to make sure that he determined whether the voter was +, –, or 0 by the end of the interview.

Chapter VII
Winning Elections

Election day activities are crucial to winning elections. To win, three functions must be performed by campaign workers in as many precincts as possible: 1) distribution of sample ballots, 2) poll watching to prevent fraud and to check on who has voted, and 3) running *plus voters* to the polls. Other activities, such as troubleshooting and visibility, support the more basic functions. If prior work has been done canvassing the precincts, a good job on election day can insure your victory and allow the general advance of political reform. But the end of a particular campaign is not necessarily the end of the group which made it possible. Permanent political organizations growing out of individual campaigns can contribute to a grassroots reform movement capable of developing new forms of democracy for our time.

A single day is the climax of each election. Months of effort are focused on this one opportunity to elect your candidate. Your workers and those of your opponents will devote from twelve to fifteen hours to the battle on election day, and when the polls close a binding verdict will have been rendered. Any votes you fail to get are lost forever. So if you don't want the hopes you have raised among the electorate to be dashed, your work on election day must insure victory for your candidate and for participatory politics.

Purpose of election day work

Three purposes are served by election day activities: 1) influencing uncommitted voters, 2) preventing election fraud, and 3) getting favorable voters to the polls. Ideally, this work is divided between three

HOW TO WIN ON ELECTION DAY

The precincts have been canvassed. We now know which voters are committed to vote for our candidate. The only task left is to make certain they do indeed vote.

There are three functions which are necessary to bring out all of our voters — distributing, checking, and running. Let us take them one at a time:

THE DISTRIBUTOR stations himself at the most strategic location (but *not closer than* 100 feet from the entrance to the polling place) where he can encounter the largest number of voters on their way to the polls. He walks up to each voter, hands him a sample ballot, and reminds him to vote for our candidate.

THE CHECKER stays inside the polling place. He seats himself near the judges' table, and marks his hard card (a list of all of the registered voters in the precinct, mounted on a piece of cardboard). As each voter fills out his application, one of the judges calls the name and address aloud, and the checker draws a red pencil line through his name.

THE RUNNER has the responsibility of getting our voters to the polls. At about 9:00 A.M. the Weisberg precinct captain checks his list of plus (Weisberg) voters against the checker's hard card, to see which plus voters have not as yet voted. (*No one* but the Weisberg workers must be allowed to see the "plus" list.) The precinct captain then fills out runner's slips for about ten or fifteen plus voters and hands them to the runner. The runner goes out into the precinct, knocks on the doors, and reminds these voters to be sure to go to the polls today. If no one is home, the slip should be scotch-taped to the door or shoved under the door. When the runner returns, the captain will have some more slips written out, and the runner once again goes out to remind these voters. Running voters in the morning should be continued until all plus voters who have not yet appeared have been contacted.

This process should be repeated again at about 1:30 P.M., 3:30 P.M., 4:15 P.M., and 5:00 P.M. If, by 5:00 P.M., there are still many pluses who have not yet voted, then even the precinct captain and the checker must go after the remaining plus voters.

In other words, every effort should be made to bring out *every* plus voter. *Running is the most important part of the entire campaign. Elections are won or lost on election day, and determined and persistent running will win the election for our candidate.*

different types of election day workers, but in understaffed precincts each worker may have to perform several functions. The three workers are 1) *the distributor* who passes out sample ballots to voters on their way to the polls, 2) the *poll watcher* or *checker* who observes the opening, operation, and closing of the polls while keeping track of exactly who has voted, and 3) the *runner* who goes door-to-door reminding plus voters to vote. Of these three functions, running is by far the most crucial to a winning campaign. As the written instructions of the Weisberg campaign conclude. "Elections are won or lost on Election Day, and determined and persistent running will win the election for our candidate."[38] At least in the opinion of Mark Perlberg, the Weisberg 44th Ward Coordinator interviewed in *By the People,* running was responsible for the Weisberg victory,[39]

Posters put up near the polling place and leaflets handed out by the distributor who encourages each voter to vote for your candidate can sway ten or twenty votes in every precinct; these jobs cannot be neglected. In a close race those few extra votes can make the difference between victory and defeat. Influencing these still uncommitted voters is important enough that you will have the company of the opposing precinct captains in front of the polling place. Be sure that they do not make pay-offs there and that both of you campaign the same distance from the polling place.[40] Even if you don't win large numbers of votes by distributing the type of endorsement card shown on page 138, you can keep the opposing precinct captain from winning them by default. The endorsement card should demonstrate the wide range of endorsements your candidate has received and should also show the appropriate lever to pull on the voting machine if there are so many offices up for election on the same day that the voter might be confused.

Many independents in machine-dominated cities like Chicago are more fearful of election fraud than they are concerned about running or distributing sample ballots. This is one reason independents lose so many elections. Poll watching to insure that votes are not stolen is a defensive action — it means your opponent will not get votes he doesn't deserve, but it doesn't produce a single vote for your candidate. Political parties do not stay dominant solely through their ability

elect
Dick Simpson Alderman February 23rd.

Endorsed by:

Chicago Tribune
Sun Times
Daily News
Chicago Today
Alderman William Singer
State Representative Bruce Douglas
State Representative Arthur Telcser
Constitutional Convention delegate Bernard Weisberg
Independent Voters of Illinois
Independent Precinct Organization
Independent Democratic Coalition
44th Ward Republican Organization
Committee for an Effective City Council
Chicago Circle Federation of Teachers, Local 1627 (AFT)
United Auto Workers/Reg. 4
Political Action Committee—Chicago Council—American Federation of Government Employees (AFL-CIO)

Dick Simpson:

An extraordinary candidate

- An award-winning teacher at the University of Illinois, Phd., and a Ford Foundation Fellow.
- Steering committee member, Campaign Against Pollution.
- Active in the fight against 4 + 1's
- Founder of the Independent Precinct Organization
- Introduced citizen's ordinance to remove politics from School Board appointments.
- Supported community stand on urban renewal.
- Pledged to maintain a full-time ward office to help all citizens obtain city services.

Elect Dick Simpson Alderman.
Vote February 23rd. (You do not have to declare your party.)

This is the Election! There will be no run-off.
You can take this card into the polling place with you.

to steal elections. Party precinct captains work year after year meeting needs of some voters in their precincts. Because they help constituents, they can deliver votes on election day. Therefore, you must do a better job in getting your voters to the polls if you are going to win. You must first win the election through work in the precincts, before worrying about the possibility of losing through fraud.

Independents usually lose because they haven't worked the precincts; election results are more often incorrectly reported because of honest errors rather than through intentional fraud. Nonetheless, there may be as many as ten per cent of the precincts where as many as a thousand votes may be stolen. If you lose by less than a thousand votes, it is tragic to think you could have won if the stealing had been prevented.

The entire electoral process, at present, favors party candidates over independents — it is easier to cast a straight party vote than to vote for separate independent candidates; many voters are affected by party identity; and independents have no formal representation among the election judges. Add to the inherent advantages of party candidates, blatant favoritism such as Paul Powell's ballot rigging in Illinois, or the unwillingness of the Cook County Elections Commission to honor voter challenges by independents, and independent candidates begin the election with a very definite handicap of several hundred lost votes. There are four ways to redress the balance: 1) law suits, 2) state constitutional reform, 3) amendments to the state election code and 4) simply getting more votes for independent candidates. A law suit challenging Paul Powell's ballot rigging was effective in the Weisberg election in permanently eliminating the problem of ballot position for independents in Illinois. Throughout the campaign such vigilance against unfair practices can mean more votes on election day. Constitutional reform and amendments to the election code are also helpful, but very slow to be instituted and unlikely to help any particular candidate for public office. By far the surest technique is to beat the other candidate by earning enough votes to overcome your initial handicaps.

Most vote fraud on election day is perpetrated by four methods: 1) stuffing the ballot box or voting machine with false votes, 2) improper voter instructions and "assistance" by election judges, 3) buying votes, and 4) recording inaccurate election results. The best protection against such vote fraud is an alert poll watcher:

> Poll watching is the only known means of safeguarding honest, democratic elections on election day. Your responsibility as a poll watcher is to detect and report any misconduct in the polling place. *You, as a poll watcher, are responsible for any errors that are made in the conduct of the election in your polling place if you do not call adequate attention to them.* Poll watching is very serious and important job.
>
> *You can be an effective poll watcher only if you are adequately informed.* When you accepted the responsibility of being a poll watcher, you accepted also the responsibility of becoming informed. Therefore, *before* election day, you should know:
>
> 1. Correct election procedures
> 2. Your rights
> 3. Your duties . . .
>
> Your effectiveness as a poll watcher depends upon you being *more informed than the Judges of Election.*[41]

Stuffing the ballot box doesn't seem to happen today as often as it once did. The penalties are stiff and it is relatively easy to detect. If the polls go unwatched, however, there is danger that this method of fraud will be used. In precincts using voting machines, additional votes for a candidate may be obtained by voting numerous times either before the polls open, during a lull, or after the polls have theoretically closed. In precincts using paper ballots, a "paper ballot chain" can be employed. The precinct captain or campaign worker steals the first ballot and marks it appropriately. He gives it to a voter with the promise of several dollars if he will vote with it. The voter goes into the polling booth and pulls the curtain. Then he takes the marked ballot from one pocket and puts the unmarked ballot in the other. After voting with the precinct captain's marked ballot, he takes the unmarked ballot back to the captain and receives his payoff. The precinct captain then marks the new ballot and the "chain" begins again. To break the "chain," a poll watcher must first detect that it is being used. Then he must enlist the aid of the election judges and policeman in searching voters who may have the marked ballot. If the judges will not cooperate, outside election observers from the Election Commission, State's Attorney's Office, or the Department of Justice must be called.

More insidious than "paper ballot chains" is improper voter "assistance" by election judges. Some election judges and even some precinct captains simply vote for citizens under the pretext of giving them assistance. Only a handicapped or illiterate citizen may have a judge actually pull levers on the voting machine for them — and only if a signed affidavit is presented. Other voters may ask for instructions either on the voting machine model or on the large voting machine. Any such instructions must be given in the presence of at least one Democratic and one Republican judge in full view of the poll watchers and should not prejudice for whom the citizen will vote.

Finally, there is the old tried and true method of vote stealing developed by such legendary politicians as Bathhouse John Coughlin and Hinky Dink Kenna.[42] Simply buy the votes you need to win. Now buying votes is not as easy as it might appear — there is an art to it. In unguarded precincts a captain can just stand outside the door of the polling place and give money to voters on their way in or out. But a wiser captain will put the money in a match book and hand those to voters or slip the money to voters with a handshake which is harder to detect. A really good precinct captain disdains even these methods. Instead he sets up an account at the pub, a cafe, or grocery store. Then voters do not get cash but are given so much in groceries, drinks, or food. The only giveaway of this fraud is a steady stream of voters leaving the polling place and going directly to the pay-off place.

If undetected, all of these methods can cause your candidate to lose a sizable number of votes on election day. However, recording the vote tallies incorrectly may cause even greater losses. To prevent such errors, two poll watchers are needed. One watcher stands behind the judge who opens the voting machines, the other sits with the judges recording the figures. The first watcher makes sure that the votes are read properly off the machines, the second that they are properly recorded. In the primary election in which Weisberg ran, several precincts were incorrectly reported. Weisberg filed a lawsuit which caused two of them to be recounted and found errors amounting to sixty-eight "stolen" votes. In a recount of a 1932 Chicago election twenty-nine percent of the ballot boxes opened showed evidence of fraud.[43]

Election day scheduling

Election day is crucial. It doesn't matter how many potential voters support your candidate if they don't show up at the polls. It doesn't matter how many citizens vote for your candidate if their votes are not fairly counted. Elections are only won if you can get enough workers for election day, train them well, and place them so as to get the maximum number of votes.

At those coffees begun so long ago you will remember that many people promised that they would work election day. Furthermore, by this time you should have a large precinct structure as well as other campaign substructures where volunteers are already at work. Each of these people — those working and those promised — must be called and asked to work election day. Area chairmen schedule all their current precinct workers first — trying particularly to get precinct captains to volunteer to work the entire day or at least to work in the morning when the polls open or in the evening when the polls close, or both. The all-day worker is needed to direct the election day work in each precinct. Extra workers are particularly needed at morning and evening because more voters vote before and after work than in the middle of the day; moreover, the polls must be closely watched when they are opened and closed if fraud is to be prevented.

As area chairmen schedule their precinct workers, a special set of volunteers in the headquarters using a special bank of phones begin calling all potential election day workers from pledge cards, the master campaign file, organization membership lists, and your candidate's petitions. In a campaign like Weisberg's, eight hundred to a thousand election day workers are needed. With each call, a special effort is made to get people to volunteer, first, to work at all on election day, then to work the hours of greatest need, and, last of all, to work as many hours as possible. The callers are carefully trained and follow instructions like those used in my campaign (page 144). In the week before the election, all election day workers — those assigned by area chairmen and those obtained by phone calls from headquarters — are carefully coordinated to give maximum coverage. As with precinct work, two principles must be considered. No precinct can go completely uncovered, but must be watched and worked at least in the morning and evening. On the other hand, every precinct which has been canvassed and in which very many plus voters reside must be manned by runners, checkers, and distributors if those votes are to be cast and counted. The need for coverage in every precinct must be balanced against the need for in-depth coverage in many already canvassed precincts.

Workers are assigned precinct by precinct on election day schedules which look something like the sheet used for precinct 43 in my campaign (page 145). Assigning hundreds of workers may well take the precinct coordinator and election day scheduler at least twelve hours. But when the work is completed, an assignment sheet (page 146) is prepared for each single election day worker and put in the training kits.

Training session

On the weekend before the election a training session or, if there are sufficient workers to justify it, several training sessions are held to prepare election day workers for the tasks they will perform and to insure that they will live up to their own commitments. For each precinct a single sack contains all necessary materials: plus list, additional poll lists, posters, buttons, leaflets, written instructions, assignment sheets, and report forms. At the meeting, oral instructions for

CITIZENS FOR SIMPSON INSTRUCTIONS FOR ELECTION DAY CALLERS

Elections are won or lost on election day. To win, we must have maximum coverage in the polling places. Your task is to get us the greatest possible number of man-hours for election day. This can be done if you follow the following steps when making calls:

1. Introduce yourself and say for whom you are calling. "Hello. My name is Joan Smith. I am a volunteer worker for Citizens For Dick Simpson. We are working to elect Dick Simpson Alderman of the new 44th Ward."
2. Ask the person if he can give us some help on election day, Tuesday, February 23rd. If the answer is yes, ask if he can give that entire day (from 5:45 A.M. through the count—about 7:00 P.M.). Explain the necessity of having workers at the polling place throughout the day.
3. If the worker cannot possibly work all day, ask if he can give us at least ten hours. If not ten, then perhaps eight. In other words, try to *get as many hours as possible.*
4. If the person can give only a few hours, first priority is 5:45 to 9:00 A.M., second priority is from 3:00 P.M. through the count.
5. Never turn anyone down no matter how few hours they can give, but try to squeeze as much time as possible from each person.
6. After you have a commitment from the person, *make sure that every question on the card is answered.* Also, remind the person that we are having a meeting of all election day workers on Sunday, February 21st. We will send him a reminder.
7. Tell the person that he may not get his final assignment until right before election day.
8. The three basic jobs that must be performed in each precinct on election day are:
    1. *Checking and poll watching* - checking off the names of people who have come in to vote and overseeing the polling place to see that proper procedures are followed.
    2. *Passing* - handing out literature to every voter before he gets to the polling place.
    3. *Running* - reminding plus and zero voters to vote.

GOOD LUCK!

ELECTION DAY ASSIGNMENT - TUESDAY, FEBRUARY 23

NAME Paul Kovich

ADDRESS 6052 Harding

HOME TELEPHONE 583-6947 OFFICE TELEPHONE ____________

YOU ARE ASSIGNED TO WORK IN AREA A PRECINCT 43

YOU ARE SCHEDULED TO WORK FROM:

5:30 AM TO Count. If at all possible, please try to come earlier and stay later. Your help is really needed to win this election.

THE POLLING PLACE TO WHICH YOU ARE TO REPORT IS LOCATED AT:

1516 W. Roscoe

WHEN YOU ARRIVE AT THE POLLING PLACE, SEE

Yourself

YOUR PRECINCT CAPTAIN IS Yourself

AND HIS/HER TELEPHONE NUMBER IS ____________

CITIZENS FOR SIMPSON 1045 W. Belmont 525-6034

Citizens for Dick Simpson
1045 W. Belmont
ELECTION DAY SCHEDULE

Telephone: 525-6034
February 23, 1971

Ward 44 Area A Precinct 43 Polling Place 1516 W. Roscoe

Precinct Captain Paul Kovich Home Phone 583-6947 Office ________

5:30 am.	
6 - 7	Paul Kovich, 6052 N. Harding, 583-6947; Leonard Cardella, 1507 Addison, 472-6462; Bill Hastings, 3033 N. Sheridan, 248-4623
7 - 8	Pat Tonn, 3416 N. Janssen, 929-1473; Dick Day, 766 Rogers, 262-1499; Mary Brinningham, 1417 W. Roscoe, 281-5503
8 - 9	
9 - 10	
10 - 11	
11 - 12	
12 - 1	
1 - 2	Jean Berger, 3428 N. Janssen, 929-1473
2 - 3	Mary Whaten, 1439 W. Roscoe, 549-0183
3 - 4	Dick Day
4 - 5	
5 - 6	Ruth Shriman, 421 W. Melrose, 477-4270
count	

election day work are given, the candidate speaks, materials are handed out and then, if possible, poll watchers are given the opportunity to practice voting and locating various counters on a voting machine. If possible, later on the same afternoon or evening each area chairman will call a meeting or party in his or her home to reinforce what the workers learned at the larger training session, to answer questions more fully, to make a final check on preparations, and to give the workers a sense of being part of a team effort. Through both the large training sessions and the area parties, morale of the workers is boosted for the final push towards victory.

The day before

The day before the election, precinct workers visit all their *plus voters* and give them an election day leaflet or reminder slip with both the candidate's name and the lever number to pull to vote for him. This reminds voters to vote and tells them how to vote for your candidate. Anyone who isn't home can be reminded by leaving the slip in the mailbox or under the door. If additional time remains after all the *plus voters* have been alerted, you can spend a few minutes talking with the most promising *zero voters* to see if any can be converted to vote for your candidate.

The night before the election in the better-funded and better-staffed campaigns a group of high school and college students are brought together to go throughout the district placing up your candidate's posters — on main streets, around polling places, at major intersections. This activity is directed by the visibility chairman and begins with a pep talk by the candidate. The real effect of this blitz is to bolster the morale of your workers, to discourage your opponents, and, by sheer visual repetition, to make voters aware of your candidate on election day. It cannot be done much before election day because your opponent's workers will tear posters down very quickly.

Election day

Election day begins for a handful of volunteers with the visibility blitz at 2:00 A.M. As the students finish their job at 3:00 or 4:00 A.M., the precincts remain unmanned. At 5:00 A.M. the new day begins as workers throughout the district arise and prepare to do battle. Precinct captains and volunteers arrive at each polling place in the district between 5:30 and 5:45 A.M. After nailing up campaign posters along the walks leading to the polling place, at least one of your workers goes inside, introduces himself to the judges, shows his poll watcher credentials if necessary, and watches the opening of the polls. As each machine is readied, he reads the "public counter" on the side of the voting machine to make sure that each counter registers 000 — no votes yet cast. He also records the number on the "private counter" at the back of the machine which gives the total number of votes cast in previous elections on this machine. If all "public counters" register zero, then the first step in insuring a fair election has been taken. If any machine does not register zero, then the Election Commission must be called to repair the machine and no votes can be cast on it until repairs are completed. In paper ballot precincts, poll watchers make sure that the ballots are still bound and unopened and that none of them are missing.

To many workers' surprise the machines do usually read zero and the election begins without incident. By 6:00 A.M., five election judges (two of one party and three of the other) are seated behind the desks as voters begin to arrive. A policeman is there to carry out the orders of these judges. A number of poll watchers and precinct captains working for various contenders are also present. The election judges have complete authority over the conduct of the election in each precinct. They should be treated with respect and courtesy, since it will do your candidate no good to have his workers thrown out of the polling place. If there are problems, a call to the campaign headquarters will bring a troubleshooter (usually a lawyer or campaign staff member) to back up your demand or test the rules. As a poll watcher your first job is to stay in the polls, not to be thrown out for causing trouble. Thus, you can suggest to the judges how you believe a situation should be handled, reinforcing your request with citations from the judge's handbook. If they fail to take your suggestion, the troubleshooter is called to handle the problem and you continue your role as a watcher.

By 7:00 A.M. the number of voters increases slightly and the distributors out front of the polling place are kept busy handing out literature and trying to keep the opposition from tearing down the posters. By 9:00 A.M. most voters will have gone to work, so the number of citizens going to the polls slows to a trickle. In many precincts, one of the campaign volunteers will begin to visit the homes of *plus voters,* encouraging them to come and vote or leaving reminder slips if they are not at home. In other precincts, that process will not begin until two or three o'clock in the afternoon. If the precinct has a busy bus stop, an additional volunteer may be stationed there to remind voters to vote before they leave for work.

All morning the checker or poll watcher inside the polls has been carefully drawing lines through names on a precinct poll list as each voter casts his ballot. A voter comes into the polling place, signs an affidavit which two judges check against names of eligible voters in the precinct binder; if the voter's name is found, the judges call it out in a loud voice so that poll watchers may also check it. No challenge being made, the voter proceeds to the voting booth, casts his vote and leaves. During slack periods, the checker compares his precinct poll list with his plus list, which has been kept safely in his pocket until now, and makes out "runner slips" for *plus voters* yet to vote. These are the slips that guide the "runners" as they convince voters to come to the polls.

Thus, ten hours pass. By four o'clock, the number of voters increases as they visit the polls after work. And at 5:45 P.M. the two poll watchers assigned to watch the count are inside waiting for the polls to close at exactly 6:00 P.M. The last voter leaves, the voting machines are opened at the back, and the results are shown. Watchers (following instructions like those given in the Weisberg campaign, page 151) carefully check the public and private counters again to be sure their tallies match and watch with anticipation and dread while the votes for their candidate and his opponents are read aloud, recorded, and totalled. As soon as the judges have completed and sealed their reports in long manila envelopes and the poll watchers have filled out their own reports on forms like the one on page 152, they rush back to headquarters to hand in these reports and to share in the victory celebration. If the judges make an error or their reports are later falsified, the poll watchers' records make future legal action possible.

After months of effort, the victory party can be a very exciting and satisfying experience. The spirit of camaraderie as well as the beer, the laughter, and the sense of accomplishment are heady stuff. Even a losing campaign can be important if people have come together to participate in elections for the first time and can see for themselves that winning is a real possibility in the next election. A successful party in victory or defeat should provide refreshments, reports of election results, and a final appearance of the candidate. Win or lose, the workers need to come away from the evening with a sense of pride in what they have accomplished and a dedication to remain active in future campaigns.

Results in the Weisberg campaign

The election results for the Weisberg campaign can be quickly told. In brief, Bernard Weisberg won and served as a delegate to the Illinois Constitutional Convention. As Table 6 demonstrates, his victory was less complete in the primary than in the run-off election and less impressive in the 48th ward, where he lost, and in the 44th Ward, which he carried by a small margin, than in the 46th Ward, where he won handily.

In politics a key question is always who won and who lost. But much more was at stake in the Weisberg election than the selection of a single public official period. First of all, a dozen independent delegates were elected around the state and were able to play a major role in the convention. Newspapers claimed that independents held a balance of power between the Chicago Democrats and the downstate Republicans. Numerically, they did, but their main contribution was not through the control of a dozen votes. Independents on the various committees played a major role in raising fundamental questions about each article of the constitution and helping to draft the final

LET'S NOT BE COUNTED OUT

The polls close promptly at 6:00 P.M. Anyone who is either voting or waiting in line is allowed to complete his vote, but no one must be permitted to enter the polling place after six o'clock.

When the last voter has left, the count begins. The machines are unlocked and the tally sheets are opened.

If two Weisberg workers are present for the count, one of them should station himself at the back of the machines *where he can read the figures.* As the judge calls out the figures by number (the candidates' names do not appear on the back of the machine) our worker should check to make certain that the figures are being called correctly, and then copy them on his report sheet. If the judge accidentally calls the figures incorrectly, call it to her attention *immediately.*

The other Weisberg volunteer should stand alongside or behind the judge who is entering the figures on the tally sheet. Be sure that she copies the figures exactly as the other judge calls them out, and records them in the proper column. If she copies incorrectly, call it to her attention *immediately.*

After the machines have been locked and re-sealed, and after the tally book has been sealed, then phone in your report to our office and come in for the *Victory party.*

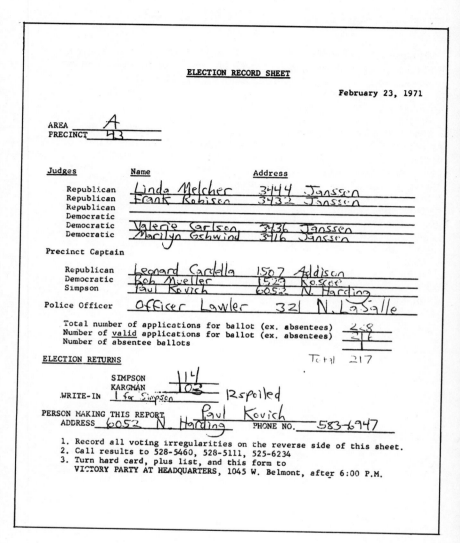

ELECTION RECORD SHEET

February 23, 1971

AREA A
PRECINCT 43

Judges	Name	Address
Republican	Linda Melcher	3444 Janssen
Republican	Frank Robison	3432 Janssen
Republican		
Democratic		
Democratic	Valerie Carlson	3436 Janssen
Democratic	Marilyn Gschwind	3416 Janssen
Precinct Captain		
Republican	Leonard Cardella	1507 Addison
Democratic	Bob Mueller	1529 Kosser
Simpson	Paul Kovich	6052 N. Harding
Police Officer	Officer Lawler	321 N. LaSalle

Total number of applications for ballot (ex. absentees) 218
Number of valid applications for ballot (ex. absentees) 216
Number of absentee ballots 1

ELECTION RETURNS Total 217

SIMPSON 114
KARGMAN 103
WRITE-IN 1 for Simpson 12 spoiled

PERSON MAKING THIS REPORT Paul Kovich
ADDRESS 6052 N. Harding PHONE NO. 583-6947

1. Record all voting irregularities on the reverse side of this sheet.
2. Call results to 528-5460, 528-5111, 525-6234
3. Turn hard card, plus list, and this form to VICTORY PARTY AT HEADQUARTERS, 1045 W. Belmont, after 6:00 P.M.

document submitted to the voters. Without the independents, the new Illinois Constitution would have been much worse. So while less than a model constitution was produced, a document significantly better than the 1870 Illinois Constitution was ratified by the voters.

Secondly, Bernard Weisberg was the first independent ever to win an election in his district, with the exception of that part of the 44th Ward which had a few months previously elected William Singer as alderman. Immediately following Weisberg's victory another independent, Bruce Douglas, was elected as state representative of the 11th District. Coupled with the able Democratic and Republican representatives from that district, the 11th District now has the most innovative and fair-minded representatives in the state. In 1971 Bill Singer was reelected by a landslide vote and I was elected alderman in a neighboring ward by a margin of fifteen hundred votes. There is no reason to believe that future victories will not occur in the district now that its history of dogmatic party control has been reversed.

Finally, Weisberg's victory, along with those of other independent candidates, signalled a major growth of participatory politics in Chicago. With the spread of independent victories to the north side of Chicago, participatory politics broke loose from its previous geographical confines and became a threat to continued control of city politics by the Democratic machine. The Chicago machine will not be destroyed immediately, but the erosion is underway and by 1975 or 1979 Chicago may well have a new mayor and far-reaching political reforms. As the Weisberg workers concluded in *By the People:*

> It is going to mean new kinds of candidates . . . .[44]
>
> . . . this is sort of like the beginning, I hope of a tidal wave. We are beginning to win significantly elsewhere, not only here . . . .[45]
>
> It means a total reformation, I think, of politics in Chicago. It shows that the mayor has lost his touch with what the people of this city want. And we're on the road . . . .[46]

Table 6

Election Results in the 11th State Senatorial District Contest to Elect Delegates to the Illinois Constitutional Convention, 1969

WARD	CANDIDATES							
	Tuchow	Weisberg	Hennigan	Harvey	Ball	Graham	Mages	Tunis
	PRIMARY							
44th	3202	3354	2636	1680	1233	1655	170	184
46th	3209	4605	3212	2367	1859	1737	350	272
48th	3604	1991	2521	1057	1380	1166	157	155
TOTAL	10,015	9,950	8,369	5,104	4,472	4,558	677	611
	RUN-OFF ELECTION							
44th	4218	4991	3739	4365	....	....	......	......
46th	4327	6943	5669	5544	....	....	......	......
48th	4973	3367	3763	2900	....	....	......	......
TOTAL	13,518	15,301	13,171	12,809	....	....	......	......

> What it means is that a lot of people in this city are growing up, and people working together for principles are showing that they're mature enough and steadfast enough to build a democracy the way a democracy ought to be built. And we don't have to take the dictates of a lot of miserable patronage-style politicians who have been choking this city and wrecking this city for three generations. We're getting to be too good for them, the people of this city. We're growing up.[47]

Staying together

After battling a single election, you will gain a deep appreciation for one virtue of a permanent political organization. Beginning campaigns with trained leaders and experienced volunteers makes elections much easier to win. To start to build a campaign organization from scratch every time an election rolls around — without any continuity and without a mechanism for selecting the best candidate — is a hopeless task. Thus, for consistently electing good men to public office a permanent organization is essential.

However, a permanent organization dedicated to promoting participatory politics can do more than elect good men to office. For one thing, it can support the men elected and keep open the lines of communication developed during the campaign between them and their constituents. By mobilizing community support and by relaying constituent complaints, requests, and questions, a permanent organization can help newly elected officials to better represent the community and to do their job more conscientiously.

In addition to electing candidates and helping them to become good public officials, a permanent political organization makes all officials more accountable for their actions. Without such an organization, there will be a considerable temptation to make too many concessions to political bosses or political parties in order to insure reelection and to gain the party support necessary to pass more legislation. Without support and a sense of obligation to the people who elected him, your newly elected official may be less outspoken, less vigorous in his representation of the community, less independent in his voting, and less aggressive in supplying the much needed services in your district.

Another advantage of a permanent political organization is that it encourages citizen participation in government policy-making by conveying requests for new policies to the officials you have managed to elect to office. They will be particularly responsive to the requests presented by your group or citizen requests which you forward to them for action. Moreover, a permanent organization has the resources to launch lobbying efforts and major issue campaigns. By mobilizing all the citizens in your district, it can put intense pressure upon public officials. With such an effort, your demands are very likely to be granted and citizens will learn to participate in policy-making as well as electioneering.

A thorough analysis of the structures and functions of permanent independent political organizations is beyond the scope of this election handbook.[48] It is sufficient at this point merely to say that, to be effective, such organizations should be precinct-based, controlled by the membership, and active in both electoral and issue campaigns which appeal for the support of all citizens in particular political districts. I have included the charter of the Independent Precinct Organization of Chicago here so that you can study the ideas and structure of one permanent political organization committed to participatory politics. However, it must be admitted that the political history of the north side of Chicago, the committed members and capable leadership of IPO, as well as the particular campaigns which IPO members supported soon after its founding has made the creation of such an organization much easier. The principles in the IPO charter met a special need for participatory politics in Chicago. While many principles are universal and while the importance of staying together as a dedicated cadre of workers from one campaign to the next is paramount, this cannot be achieved by blindly copying the IPO. Each group must consider the principles of permanent organizations point by point and adopt only those that really meet the needs in their areas.

Building permanent organizations is an even more creative task than running a good campaign.

Such an organization is built out of the committed workers in a particular campaign. After the campaign is over, win or lose, call all the workers together and present a carefully thought out proposal for working together in future elections and creating a permanent organization. If the time is ripe and the specific proposal a good one, there will be great support for it among these campaign veterans.

The future for participatory politics

What does the future hold? In opposition to the pessimistic prophecies that all our attempts to reform the political system will fail, that a violent revolution, extensive political repression, or simply slow degeneration will be our destiny, there are alternative visions of the future. In addition to the usual hopes for internal party reform or the creation of new political parties, there is the possibility of developing a broad movement for political reform much like those of the populist or progressive eras in American history. If this movement is nurtured, existing political parties will either reform or be replaced by new independent political organizations, according to the conditions of the time. Unlike earlier attempts to reform government by the introduction of civil service or like the movements for peace or civil rights which are built around a single issue, the current reform movement must seek to create a political base built upon an informed electorate eager to participate in a more open political process than now exists.

Nationally there will continue to be presidential candidates like Eugene McCarthy, George McGovern, Fred Harris, and Harold Hughes who attempt to represent a new politics of conscience, reform, participation, and decency. The current value of such presidential campaigns and battles in the U.S. Senate and reports by presidential or political party commissions of inquiry is to sound the trumpet of change — to cause people still sleeping in villages, towns, and cities to awaken to the need for a new beginning in the centuries-old effort to create a just democracy. None of these national ventures can suc-

INDEPENDENT PRECINCT ORGANIZATION CHARTER

We believe that those who are affected by the decisions of government must be consulted by those who govern. It is the right of a citizen to have access to the instruments of power; it is his duty to learn to use them effectively and wisely. We seek to elect to public office men who will serve with wisdom and imagination, while remaining responsive to those who gave them office. We seek to build a citizenry confident in its capacity to select its leaders and to take part in the making of public policy.

The Independent Precinct Organization is a means to achieve this program for the community at large. We will serve as well to make visible a political community which is at once energetic and humane. All who have a stake in our decisions will participate in making them; all who participate will share the responsibility for implementation. By fostering responsible citizen participation in public affairs, by promoting fresh, responsive political leadership, by demonstrating in our ways of work the wisdom of popular democracy, we seek to bring about a new political order in our community.

I. MEMBERSHIP

A. A member in good standing of the Independent Precinct Organization is one who has fulfilled the responsibilities of membership for two consecutive months. Those responsibilities are:

1. A regular, sustained expenditure of time on the activities of the organization
2. A regular monthly contribution of dues in an amount to be set by the individual.

II. MEMBERSHIP ASSEMBLIES

A. The General Assembly consists of all members in good standing of the organization. The General Assembly determines the leadership, candidates, and policy of the organization as a whole.

1. The IPO Executive Committee brings to the General Assembly recommendations for persons to fill the following positions:
   a. Chairman of the General Assembly
   b. Executive Director of IPO
   c. Chairman of Commissions
   d. Chairman of Committees
2. The Commission for Electoral Action brings to the General Assembly recommendations for candidates to be supported by the organization as a whole.
3. The Commission for Community Action brings to the General Assembly recommendations for programs to be undertaken by the organization as a whole.

4. Additional nominations of leadership or candidates and suggestions for policies or programs may be made from the floor of the General Assembly. The election of leaders requires a simple majority vote; selection of candidates and policies or programs requires a two-thirds majority vote.

B. A Ward Assembly consists of all IPO members who work in that Ward's precinct organization or who reside in the Ward and regularly work on the staff, a committee or commission of IPO. The Ward Assembly determines the leadership, candidates and policies or programs of the Ward. The Ward Assembly elects two representatives from its membership to the Executive Committee. A member of a Ward Assembly who does not reside within that Ward may not serve as an elected officer or an elected representative of that Ward Assembly.

1. The Executive committee brings to the Ward Assembly recommendations for Coordinator of the Ward.
2. The Commission for Electoral Action brings to the Ward Assembly recommendations regarding Aldermanic candidates for that Ward.
3. The Commission for Community Action brings to the Ward Assembly recommendations for programs to be undertaken by that Ward.
4. Additional nominations for Ward Coordinator, Aldermanic Candidate and suggestions for policies or programs may be made from the floor of the Ward Assembly. Election of Ward Coordinator requires a simple majority vote; selection of candidates and policies or programs requires a two-thirds majority vote.
5. If a Ward decision regarding candidates or policies does not meet with the approval of the IPO Executive Committee the matter shall be brought before the next General Assembly, where a two-thirds majority vote shall be required to uphold the original decision of the Ward Assembly.

C. There shall be one membership assembly per month. Meetings of the General Assembly may alternate with those of the Ward Assemblies as the needs of the organization dictate. A quorum of one-third of the members in good standing is required to conduct business. One week's notice is required for all Assembly meetings; names of candidates to be proposed by a Commission or Committee shall be included in the notification.

III. ADMINISTRATIVE COMMITTEES

A. The IPO Executive Committee consists of the Executive Director, the Chairman of the General Assembly, the Coordinator of each Ward, two representatives elected by each Ward Assembly, the chairman of the commissions, and the chairman of the committees.

1. Members of the Executive Committee are elected for six month terms. Elections for these positions are held in November and May, or as vacancies occur.
2. The Executive Committee is responsible for implementing the policies of the General Assembly. All major policy decisions must be approved by the General Assembly or, if time does not permit prior approval, reviewed by the General Assembly at its next meeting. The Executive Committee also reviews the budget, approves major expenditures, and hires whatever staff may be necessary to implement the policies and programs of the General Assembly.

B. A Ward Committee consists of a Ward Coordinator, Area Chairman (appointed by the Executive Committee in consultation with the Ward Coordinator), and two Ward representatives to the Executive Committee.

1. The Ward Committee is responsible for implementing IPO policies within the Ward. The Ward Committee is responsible for evaluating the membership status of a worker and for suspending his voting privilege should he fail to fulfill the responsibilities of IPO membership. Any decision regarding membership may be appealed to the Executive Committee.

IV. FUNCTIONAL COMMITTEES

A. The Program Committee is responsible for planning and supervising social and educational gatherings conducted for or by the organization.

B. The Public Relations Committee is responsible for communicating political information and the programs of IPO to the public during and between election campaigns.

C. The Finance Committee is responsible for raising funds, for preparing the budget and for maintaining the financial records of IPO.

V. COMMISSIONS

A. A Commission consists of the Chairman, two representatives selected by each Ward Committee, and such other members as the Commission Chairman appoints, subject to the approval of the Executive Committee.

1. A Commission may undertake informal discussion with representatives of political parties and community organizations as part of its work; it may commit the name, workers and funds of IPO to other groups only with the consent of the General Assembly or of a Ward Assembly.

B. The Commission for Electoral Action is responsible for preparing the IPO for all election campaigns by locating potential candidates for public office and for investigating possibilities for electoral reform.

C. The Commission for Community Action is responsible for investigating the social and economic problems of the community and for proposing political means of dealing with them.

VI. RATIFICATION AND AMENDMENT OF THIS CHARTER

A. This Charter shall be ratified by a two-thirds majority of those voting at a meeting of the General Assembly.

B. A two-thirds majority of those voting at a meeting of the General Assembly shall be required to amend this Charter. Proposed amendments shall be published to the membership one month prior to the meeting at which the vote is to be taken.

ceed until a local base for participatory politics has spread across the country. Yet each wave of national reform leaves in its wake more fertile ground for local campaigns and local organizations which, as they grow, preserve the values which made the national efforts possible in the past and more likely to succeed in the future.

Many people become disappointed when their presidential candidate is defeated, their favorite senator fails to be reelected, or another commission report goes unheeded. Idealists who once believed — and who still want to believe — that participatory politics can be made to work in America turn to violence as the only solution for America's plight. Having lost every election, having been jailed for demonstrating their discontent, having listened to hundreds of worthless political promises, having seen the war on poverty fail as the war in Vietnam escalated, they have become convinced of the necessity for total, revolutionary change which can be brought about only by revolutionary war. They have failed to comprehend the true possibilities of building a local base for participatory politics.

Participatory politics is not simply a slogan. It does not come into being because someone says the words. It requires instead the development of particular institutions and processes and the opportunities for citizens to participate effectively in elections where the choice of candidates makes a difference and in government policy-making where the public is actually consulted. These electoral and issue campaigns cost time and money. They require sacrifices, but they allow people again to take part in those decisions which most affect their lives. As you have seen in this handbook, successful participatory campaigns require a knowledge of the basic mechanics of electioneering and a commitment to doing a hell of a lot of work to win.

People make the sacrifices to work in participatory campaigns because the stakes are not one more person holding public office or a particular "pay off" in money or position, or even a few new laws. What is at stake is whether our political system can be made more open and more democratic or whether tyranny and repression, in one form or another, shall prevail. Political reform is thus not a pastime or hobby, but demands a seriousness and dedication beyond that required in many vocations.

Each successful election, each issue campaign, and, most of all, each new permanent political organization contributes to our collective experience with the institutions and processes of participatory politics and builds a constituency which will assert the right to participate. Each election, issue campaign and new organization trains leaders better able to articulate visions of what America should be like and better able to organize citizens to transform our national institutions. It is too soon to know the final shape our new national politics may take, but it is not too soon to know that it will be born in the local struggles in the Chicagos, Bloomingtons, Madisons, and Houstons of our nation.

No matter what happens in terms of the general movement, you can play a vital role in shaping the future at least of your own community. You can elect outstanding public officials and help to solve your own community problems. You can serve as an organizer, recruiting fellow citizens to the cause of political reform and coordinating their actions in different political campaigns. You can serve as a spokesman for participatory politics, helping to give specific shape and form to the more general visions.

A new form of participatory politics is being born. Whether it is to flourish or die depends on how many citizens are willing to dedicate themselves to sustaining and perfecting it. Our ultimate success or failure may well depend upon your choice to join with us. There is no greater challenge than developing for our time new forms of democracy. There can be no greater condemnation than to fail to take up this challenge. For what we do in America's towns and cities today lays the foundation for a new national politics of conscience and participation tomorrow.

Questions

1. Of the three functions of election day activities which is the most essential to a winning campaign? Why? pp. 135, 137

2. What are the chief methods of election fraud and how may they

be guarded against? pp. 139-140.
3. How are workers obtained and scheduled for election day? pp. 142-143.
4. What were the results in the Weisberg election and what did they mean in terms of the Constitutional Convention, future independent victories in the district, and participatory politics generally? pp. 150, 153.
5. What are the reasons to stay together in a permanent political organization after a campaign is over? pp. 155-154.

Workshop Exercise

As a concluding exercise you may want to analyze the differences between "participatory politics" and previous styles of campaigning. Put the following chart on a blackboard or poster:

	McCARTHY-KENNEDY CAMPAIGNS, 1968	OLD POLITICS*	PARTICIPATORY POLITICS
CANDIDATES			
PUBLIC RELATIONS			
PRECINCT ORGANIZATION			

Then ask the group to give characteristics of candidates, public relations, and precinct organization under each type of politics. After most characteristics are listed step back and ask someone to summarize the differences and whether or not it is worth fighting to bring participatory politics into existence in your community.

*In Chicago we use the "Daley Machine" as an example of "Old politics." Elsewhere more local examples should be used.

Appendix I

The ideal format for training workshops would seem to be: 1) to read the handbook beforehand, 2) to see the film *By the People** in its entirety at the first meeting of the workshop, and 3) to divide the workshop into several discussion sessions organized around key chapters of the handbook. Thus, the suggested timetable would be something like the following:

WORKSHOP TIMETABLE

I. PARTICIPATORY POLITICS (Approximately 2 hours)

A. Brief introduction
B. *By The People* is shown
C. General discussion of film

II. BUILDING AN ORGANIZATION (45 minutes)

A. An experienced campaign manager or volunteer coordinator speaks to group
B. Reshowing of recruitment process at Weisberg Coffee (Optional)

III. GETTING KNOWN (45 minutes)

A. Break down into discussion groups and attempt to develop theme and schedule for an imaginary or real campaign as an example

* William Mahin and Dick Simpson, *By The People: A Study of Independent Politics — Chicago, 1969.*

B. Reshowing of public relations discussion in film (Optional)

IV. PREPARING FOR BATTLE (45 minutes)

A. Talk by a former precinct coordinator
B. Reshowing of registration instructions & drive (Optional)

V. CANVASSING (45 minutes)

A. Role playing of door-to-door canvassing in small discussion groups
B. Discussion in small groups of plus, minus and zero voter system

VI. ELECTION DAY WORK (30 minutes)

A. Brief discussion of roles on election day
B. Reshowing election day for the Weisberg campaign (Optional)

VII. GENERAL DISCUSSION OF POLITICAL GOALS AND STYLES (30 minutes)

Such a workshop would thus take only six hours and could be completed in a single weekend afternoon, completed as part of a longer conference or presented in seven weekly evening sessions. Depending on which way the workshop is scheduled, appropriate breaks for meals or relaxation will need to be added.

Appendix II

Sample of Candidate's Schedule

January 31 Sunday

10:30 A.M.	Attend church and coffee afterwards The Parish of Reconciliation 1655 W. School
12:00 P.M.	Strategy meeting at campaign headquarters
2:45 P.M.	Press conference Sheraton Chicago Lake Michigan, 8th fl. (Endorsement by several former delegates to the State Constitutional Convention)
7:00 P.M.	George Newton (coffee) 522 Roscoe
7:30 P.M.	Nancy Moss (coffee) 3330 N. Lake Shore
8:00 P.M.	Canvass training session speech Headquarters
8:45 P.M.	Berg family (coffee) 2915 Sheffield

February 1 Monday

7:30 A.M.	Bus stop handshaking (Roscoe and Sheridan)
10:00 A.M.	Interview with David Anderson at headquarters for Lerner Newspapers
2:00 P.M.	Walking tour in Precinct 31
7:45 P.M.	Aaron and Lois Levine (coffee) 3147 N. Cambridge

8:45 P.M. Alen Silberman (coffee)
3033 Sheridan
9:45 P.M. Mr. and Mrs. Dave Silberman (coffee)
3150 Lake Shore
10:15 P.M. Spanish meeting at headquarters (speech, photographs for newspaper and mailing)

February 2 Tuesday

7:30 A.M. Diversey El stop handshaking
9:30 A.M. City Hall Election Commission press conference
10-12:00 P.M. Class at UICC
7:00 Isadore Schachter (coffee)
421 Melrose
7:30 P.M. West Lakeview Neighbors Debate
St. Luke's Church
1500 W. Belmont

February 3 Wednesday

7:30 A.M. Bus stop (Aldine and Sheridan)
9:15 A.M. Mrs. Mark Baskin
Nettelhorst PTA President
442 Aldine
(Discussion of issues)
10:30 A.M. Francis Parker
(High school assembly speech)
1-4:00 P.M. Walking tour with Father Lezak in west side precincts
1:00 P.M. Meeting with Le Moyne School Principal
851 Waveland
(Discussion of school issues)
6:30 P.M. Pat Buondin (coffee)
8:45 P.M. Bob and Kate Kestnbaum (coffee)
442 Wellington

9:45 P.M. Irv and Carol Ware (coffee)
3400 Lake Shore
10:30 P.M. Weekly steering committee meeting

February 4 Thursday

10:00 A.M. N.O.W. Press Conference
201 N. Wells
(Endorsement by National Organization of Women)
2:00 P.M. Senior Citizens Debate
Jane Addams Center, Hull House
4:30 P.M. Illinois Nurses Association cocktail party
8 S. Michigan
6:00 P.M. Dinner with Scott and Sara Jane at restaurant to raise money
7:45 P.M. Mr. and Mrs. Allen Porter (coffee)
703 Briar
8:45 P.M. Mr. and Mrs. John Light (coffee)
3430 N. Lake Shore
9:45 P.M. Mr. and Mrs. Julius Polikoff (coffee)
3180 N. Lake Shore
10:15 P.M. LUCC Board Meeting
St. Bonaventure
1615 Diversey

February 5 Friday

7:30 A.M. Belmont and Broadway bus stop
9:00 A.M. Betty Garman, Principal
Morse School, 919 Barry
1:00 P.M. Betty Fossmo (coffee)
1223 W. George
3:30-5:30 P.M. Walking Tour with Kerm Krueger
Appleton Plaza (Wells and Ashland)
5:30 P.M. Dinner with Bob Johnson, Tommy and Pat
445 W. Surf
7:00 P.M. Mrs. Bert Schenker (coffee)
468 Melrose

8:00 P.M. Mrs. Edith Bukwa (coffee)
850 Buckingham
9:15 P.M. 44th Ward Republican Organization meeting
3922 Broadway
(Endorsement by Republican Organization)

February 6 Saturday

9-12:00 P.M. Shopping center handshaking
Lincoln, Belmont and Ashland
12:00 P.M. Headquarters strategy meeting
1-3:00 P.M. Del Farm Area handshaking
3-5:00 P.M. Lincoln, Belmont and Ashland
Shopping center handshaking
2-4:00 P.M. Walking Tour Area B
7-8:00 P.M. Coffee at St. Alphonse
8:30 P.M. Swedish Engineering Club
Benefit Dinner
(play and film)

February 7 Sunday

11:00 A.M. Latin Groups
St. Sebastion's Church
1:30 P.M. Spanish meeting
1032 George
2:00 P.M. Dan Crowe (coffee)
741 Melrose
3:00 P.M. Bob and Sue Houston (coffee)
817 Wolfarm
4-7:00 P.M. Mr. and Mrs. Michael Maremont
Committee for an Effective City Council Benefit
940 Sheridan, Glencoe
(250 contr. for campaign)
7:30 P.M. Fern Zittler
1104 W. George
8:00 P.M. Temple Sholom (debate)
Brotherhood Town Hall Meeting

Notes

1. William Mahin and Dick Simpson, *By The People: A Study of Independent Politics — Chicago, 1969.* (New York: Radim Films, Inc., 17 W. 60th Street, 1970.)
2. For a review of some of the literature relating personality traits and political participation see Lester Milbrath, *Political Participation* (Chicago: Rand McNally, 1965), Chapter 3.
3. From Thucydides, *History,* Book II, Chapter VI, Section 40, as translated by Alfred E. Zimmern in *The Greek Commonwealth.* (London: Oxford University Press), p. 204.
4. Max Lerner, "Political Man Is Needed," *Chicago Sun-Times,* August 6, 1970, p. 90.
5. Several workers shown in *By The People,* Reel I.
6. Bernard Weisberg in *By The People,* Reel I.
7. Lester Milbrath, *Political Participation.* William Flanigan, *Political Behavior of the American Electorate* (Boston: Allyn and Bacon, 1968). Angus Campbell, *et. al., The American Voter* (New York: Wiley, 1964).
8. No principle or rule can be applied absolutely or unthinkingly. For instance, when I ran for alderman in 1971 under newly drawn ward boundaries, I moved into a ward adjacent to the ward in which I had previously lived. However, I did so only at the request of the citizens' search committee and I had lived on the north side of Chicago for four years.
9. William Singer, "Reflections on Campaign Techniques" (Mimeographed paper printed by Committee on Illinois Government, Chicago, 1969), p. 8.
10. In *By The People,* reports at headquarters are shown in the registration drive sequence on Reel I.
11. *By The People,* Reel I.
12. *By The People,* Reel I.
13. Bob Houston, "What Every *Great* Coffee Chairman Has to Know" (Mimeographed instructions for coffee chairmen, Bruce Dumont for State Senator Campaign, Chicago, 1970).

14. *By The People,* Reel I.
15. Hank Parkinson, *Winning Your Campaign: A Nuts-and-Bolts Guide to Political Victory* (Englewood Cliffs, New Jersey: Prentice-Hall, 1970), p. 77.
16. *By The People,* Reel I.
17. Don Rose in *By The People,* Reel I.
18. Don Rose in *By The People,* Reel I.
19. Hank Parkinson, "Publicity Is Inexpensive and Neglected," *Campaign Insight,* I, No. 3 (June, 1970), p. 8.
20. *Stevenson of Illinois Campaign Manual* (Chicago: Adlai E. Stevenson III for U.S. Senator Campaign, 1970), pp. 35-36.
21. Different stations reach different audiences. To determine if it is worth advertising on a particular station, professional public relations firms should be consulted.
22. Byron Sistler, "Political Action in Action," *IVI Bellringer* (March, 1969), p. 6.
23. Movement for a New Congress, *Vote Power* (Englewood Cliffs: Prentice-Hall, 1970), pp. 8 and 12.
24. *Ibid,* p. 27. See also pp. 14-15.
25. *Ibid,* p. 18.
26. E. E. Schattschneider, *The Semi-Sovereign People* (New York: Holt, Rinehart and Winston, 1960), p. 4.
27. *Vote Power,* p. 17.
28. Jerry Murray in *By The People,* Reel I.
29. *Vote Power,* p. 28.
30. "How To Win Elections," (Mimeographed instructions, Bernard Weisberg Campaign, Chicago, 1969). Jim Chapman, Weisberg precinct co-ordinator, adapted these instructions from those written for previous independent campaigns by Sherwin Schwartz, a staff member of the Independent Voters of Illinois
31. *Vote Power,* p. 29.
32. Jim Chapman in *By the People,* Reel I.
33. Stokely Carmichael and Charles Hamilton, *Black Power: The Politics of Liberation in America* (New York: Vintage, 1967), especially Chapter V.
34. Ed Lawrence, "Handbook for Independent Precinct Workers" (Mimeographed manual for IPO and IVI precinct workers in the 42nd Ward, Chicago, 1970), p. 3.
35. "Instructions for Telephone Canvassing," (Mimeographed instructions, Kearney campaign, Chicago, 1969).
36. James Kessler, "Running for State Political Office," in Cornelius Cotter (ed.), *Practical Politics in the United States* (Boston: Allyn and Bacon, 1969), p. 126.

37. John Kearney, "Campaign Realities," *Chicago Sun-Times,* Letter to the Editor, March 28, 1970.
38. "How to Win on Election Day," (Mimeographed instructions, Bernard Weisberg campaign, Chicago, 1969).
39. Mark Perlberg in *By the People,* Reel II.
40. According to Illinois law you should campaign at least one hundred feet from the polls. However, this law differs in other states.
41. Sandye Wexler, "So You're a Poll Watcher," (Mimeographed manual for poll watchers, Weisberg campaign, Chicago, 1969), p. 1.
42. Lloyd Wendt and Herman Kogan, *Bosses in Lusty Chicago* (Bloomington: Indiana University Press, 1967). Originally published as *Lords of the Levee* by Bobbs-Merrill in 1943.
43. Harold Gosnell, *Machine Politics: Chicago Model* (Chicago: University of Chicago Press, 1968), p. 87. First published, 1937.
44. Dick Simpson in *By the People,* Reel II.
45. Mark Perlberg in *By the People,* Reel II.
46. Marvin Rosner in *By the People,* Reel II.
47. Donald Page Moore in *By the People,* Reel II
48. See George Beam and Dick Simpson, *Strategies for Change* (Forthcoming 1972) for a discussion of strategies and institutions needed for political change, including independent political organizations.

An Annotated Bibliography

I. Voting, Participation, and Representation

Campbell, Angus *et. al.* *The American Voter.* New York: Wiley, 1964.

The first comprehensive study of voting behavior among the entire American electorate. Focusing particularly upon the 1952 and 1956 elections, the authors of *The American Voter* explain voting decisions primarily in terms of party identification, candidates and issues but they also consider other characteristics such as the socio-economic background of voters.

Key, V. O., Jr. *The Responsible Electorate.* New York: Random House, 1966.

A major study defending the rationality of the voter. Drawing upon voting studies of presidential elections from 1936-1960, Key argues that voters decide their party and even their candidate preferences to a great extent by their stands on crucial issues of the period.

Leuthold, David. *Electioneering in a Democracy.* New York: Wiley, 1968.

A study of campaigns in ten congressional districts of the San Francisco Bay area during 1962. Leuthold is concerned with gathering and application of resources in campaigns and concludes that 1) declaration of candidacy, 2) party backing, 3) issue stands, 4) support of nonpolitical groups, 5) money and 6) campaign volunteers are essential to winning votes.

Milbrath, Lester. *Political Participation.* Chicago: Rand McNally, 1965.

A summary of existing political science literature on political participation, including a model of participation derived inductively from the findings. Probably the best single book available on the subject, *Political Participation* also contains a good bibliography referring to the major works in the field at the time of publication.

Snowiss, Leo. "Congressional Recruitment and Representation," *American Political Science Review,* LX (September, 1966), pp. 627-639.

A comparison of different types of congressional representation from the Chicago metropolitan area according to type of political party organization and candidate recruitment procedures. The author's thesis is that different types of candidates emerge from the inner city, outer city and suburban areas, not only because of socio-economic differences, but because of differences in the type of party control in each area.

II. Political Party Machines

Costikyan, Edward. *Behind Closed Doors.* New York: Harcourt, Brace and Jovanovich, 1966.

An up-to-date description of practical politics in a previously machine-controlled city where for 14 years Edward Costikyan was a Tammany Hall precinct captain and political leader. *Behind Closed Doors* provides a thoughtful discussion of party politics and the "good government" alternative from the perspective of a regular party politician.

Flynn, Edward, *You're the Boss.* New York: Viking Press, 1947.

A defense of machine politics as "indispensable" because of its function of representing voters and the services it provides. The author is the former Boss of the Bronx and former Chairman of the Democratic National Committee. The book is perhaps most notable for its distinction between good and bad machines and its classic description of local political party meetings.

Gosnell, Harold. *Machine Politics.* Chicago: University of Chicago Press, 1968. First published 1937.

This is one of the best studies of machine politics made by a social scientist. Focusing on Chicago from 1928-1936, Gosnell examines the party workers and the parties themselves during a time of severe economic change only to discover that, while the party in power changed, the characteristics of the political system in Chicago did not. He further analyzes voting behavior of the period especially with reference to the influence of the newspapers upon voting. A foreword by Theodore Lowi and a postscript by the author recounts the Chicago experience between 1937 and 1967 and places the findings in a more universal framework.

Reum, Walter and Gerald Mattran. *Politics From the Inside Up.* Chicago: Follett, 1966. (Paperback edition by Dutton.)

A humorous book detailing twenty-five rules on how to build a successful political career. It includes how to join the party, which party to join, how to conduct your campaigns, what to do once elected, and how to be elected to higher positions. Not only is it a most readable book, but the suggestions on how to succeed reveal the way a political party actually works instead of the usual "good government" explanations of how they should work.

Riordan, William. *Plunkitt of Tammany Hall.* New York: Dutton, 1963

In a set of speeches made from a shoe shine stand in City Hall, Tammany Hall boss George Washington Plunkitt, gives his personal account of the Tammany machine and the philosophical principles upon which it was based. A frank account, in Plunkitt's words, of "what all practical politicians think but are afraid to say."

III. Winning Traditional Party and Public Relations Elections

Anderson, Walt. *Campaigns: Cases in Political Conflict.* Pacific Palisades, California: Goodyear, 1970.

An historical treatment of fourteen campaigns ranging from the Lincoln-Douglas campaign up to the New Hampshire campaign of Eugene McCarthy, *Campaigns* points up the differences in campaigns in various regions and at various times in our history, as well as emphasizing candidates, oratory, issues and events which influenced the outcome.

Bullitt, Stimson, *To Be A Politician.* Garden City, New York: Doubleday, 1961.

The book is divided into four sections covering politics as a profession, campaigns, qualities present in the best politicians and the need for leadership from among the leisure class. Stimson's treatment of campaigning includes a thoughtful consideration of changing methods and of the continued need for organizations such as political parties. It is not a nuts-and-bolts discussion, but a general overview of the process.

Chamber of Commerce of the United States. *Action Course in Practical Politics.* Washington, D.C.: Chamber of Commerce, 1959.

Eight pamphlets are provided for eight separate sessions in which various aspects of practical politics can be studied and discussed. The bias is toward participation through the normal political party channels. The pamphlets cover the following topics: 1) The Individual in Politics, 2) Political Party Organization, 3) The Political Precinct, 4) The Political Campaign, 5) Political Clubs, 6) The Political Leader's Problems, 7) Political Meetings, and 8) Businessmen in Politics.

Fetridge, William Harrison. *The Republican Precinct Worker's Manual.* Chicago: United Republican Fund of Illinois, 80 East Jackson Blvd., 1968.

Fetridge, who served as campaign manager of Robert Merriam's campaign for Mayor of Chicago in 1955 and as chairman of the Midwest Volunteers for Nixon-Lodge in 1960, has put together an extremely readable manual in the form of a dialogue between a new party volunteer and an elder statesman of the party. It answers many of the questions likely to occur to an inexperienced worker.

McGinniss, Joe. *The Selling of the President 1968.* New York: Pocket Books, 1970. First published by Trident Press, 1969.

This volume updates the normal material on electioneering to include attempts to manipulate the media to a candidate's advantage. In this case, McGinniss provides an inside story of the attempt to use the media to elect Nixon as president in 1968. It is not a handbook, but it does give detailed descriptions and contains an appendix of several scripts for various political commercials.

Nimmo, Dan. *The Political Persuaders.* Englewood Cliffs: Prentice Hall, 1970.

Treatment of new techniques of profiling the electorate and projecting the candidate through the mass media. Nimmo also presents considerable information about professional campaign managers and the successes and failures of such techniques in recent years. *Political Persuaders* is very similar to Perry's *The New Politics.*

Parkinson, Hank. *Winning Your Campaign: A Nuts-and-Bolts Guide to Political Victory.* Englewood Cliffs: Prentice Hall, 1970.

A realistic guide to modern campaign practices and most particularly to the public relations aspects such as announcing candidacy, holding press conferences, writing press releases, and campaign scheduling. It is written particularly for potential candidates, offering advice both under what conditions one should run and how to run a successful campaign. Probably the best handbook for regular party candidates available.

Perry, James. *The New Politics.* New York: Potter, 1968.
An early account of the effect of professional campaign managers using new computer technology along with television to sell candidates to the voters. The two characteristics of this style of politics are that appeals are made directly to the voters and that the techniques used to make the appeals — polling, computers, television, direct mail — should be sophisticated and scientific. Perry provides a good general description of the techniques, but only limited suggestions for running campaigns.

IV. New Politics

A. McCarthy Campaign

Herzog, Arthur. *McCarthy for President.* New York: Viking, 1969.
McCarthy for President, which describes the three McCarthy campaigns against Johnson, then Kennedy and finally Humphrey, is by one of the older and more experienced staff members. It is useful for the background on McCarthy himself as well as for its overview of the campaign. Herzog concludes that the campaign was successful in "bringing down a president in office, moving the United States toward peace in Vietnam, pulling . . . an entire generation into politics, and forcing the Democratic Party to take stock of itself . . ."

McCarthy, Eugene. *The Year of the People.* Garden City, New York: Doubleday, 1969.
The Year of the People gives McCarthy's own position on the issues, his reasons for running, and his evaluation of the campaign. While skipping over most details of campaign organization and operation, it provides a perspective not available in any of the other discussions of 1968.

Stavis, Ben. *We Were the Campaign.* Boston: Beacon Press, 1969.
This is the best of the three books on the McCarthy campaign in terms of the details of campaign organization and day-to-day decision-making. It is also successful in distinguishing between the McCarthy campaign and earlier efforts, and in telling the story of the campaign from the perspective of student volunteers. Stavis also discusses the internal campaign struggles and problems.

B. Kennedy Campaigns

Levin, Murray. *Kennedy Campaigning.* Boston: Beacon Press, 1966.

Based upon Edward Kennedy's campaign of 1962 for senator of Massachusetts, Levin's book explores the Kennedy style of campaigning, campaign organization, use of television, allocation of resources, and method of creating news.

Newfield, Jack. *Robert Kennedy: A Memoir.* New York: Bantam, 1970. First published by Dutton, 1969.

Although primarily a memoir of Robert Kennedy's life, Newfield's book covers Robert Kennedy's hesitation in running for president and his campaign. In addition to focusing upon Kennedy as a man and a politician, Newfield also describes the support which Kennedy could tap from minority groups, working class and some labor and political leaders. While not a book on campaigning, it is useful in understanding one of the most important politicians in the new politics movement.

C. Alternatives

Chester, Lewis, *et. al. An American Melodrama: The Presidential Campaign of 1968.* New York: Dell, 1969. Hardcover edition published by Viking, 1969.

The most comprehensive analysis yet made of the campaigns for president in both parties, *An American Melodrama* also considers the underlying malaise of American politics and the violent, melodramatic conclusions to the campaigns. The authors have done an outstanding job both in bringing to light innumerable details of the politics of 1968 and in putting its political events into a broader perspective.

Lamb, Karl and Paul Smith. *Campaign Decision-Making: The Presidential Election of 1964.* Belmont, California: Wadsworth, 1968.

Although not about a "new politics" campaign, *Campaign Decision-Making* raises important issues about the inherent relationship between campaign structure and campaign rhetoric or ideology. Advocates of "new politics" should be acutely aware of the defects of the Goldwater campaign of 1964, as well as the normal campaign methods of presidential candidates. This book provides important information and theories about both.

Manso, Peter (ed.). *Running Against the Machine.* Garden City, New York: Doubleday, 1969.

These readings are taken from speeches and position papers by Norman Mailer and Jimmy Breslin in their campaign for mayor and president of the City Council of New York in the 1969 Democratic primary. They ran a philosophical campaign based on "left-conservatism" and on the platform of making New York City the 51st state and returning power to the neighborhoods. Although Mailer and Breslin are two of the best known authors in America, their political campaign was never taken seriously by the press. Nonetheless, it stands as one alternative — a campaign with issue positions quite divergent from "accepted opinions" — and as such is worthy of careful study.

V. The Nuts and Bolts of Participatory Politics

Knapp, Robert. *A Manual for Precinct Workers.* Chicago: Labor Education Division, Roosevelt University, 1969. First published by Independent Voters of Illinois.

A step-by-step guide for independent precinct workers, covering all stages of a campaign from gathering petition signatures until after the election. Brief but most helpful for new workers.

Movement for a New Congress. *Vote Power.* Englewood Cliffs: Prentice Hall, 1970.

Although focusing upon preparations for the 1970 Congressional campaigns, the suggested techniques are useful in any campaign. *Vote Power* emphasizes how to choose campaigns in which to work, the specific services volunteers can perform, and how to remain politically effective after the campaign. *Vote Power* also includes appendices on marginal congressional districts, roll call votes in Congress, and registration laws in various states.

Simpson, Dick. *Independent Precinct Organization: A Programmed Textbook.* Chicago: Independent Precinct Organization, 1969. (Now out of print.)

This textbook of independent political campaigns is interesting as a precedessor to *Winning Elections* and as an experiment with a different style of presentation.

Singer, William. "Reflections on Campaign Techniques" Chicago. Mimeographed paper by Committee on Illinois Government, 1969.

A brief discussion of the roles of key campaign personnel and their relationship to the candidate in an independent campaign.

Welland, Robert and Eric Wexler. *A Campaign Manual for Independ-*

ents. Evanston, Illinois: Northwestern University Political Action Conference, 1970.

This manual prepared especially for a conference held on August 1-2, 1970 provides general discussions of running political campaigns, the various staff roles to be played, and contains many of the instructions and report forms provided in *Winning Elections.*

Wexler, Sandye. *So You're a Poll Watcher.* Chicago: Independent Precinct Organization, 1969.

This poll watcher's manual was prepared for the Weisberg campaign and contains a detailed discussion of Illinois election laws and poll watching in Illinois.

VI. Alternative Visions of the Future or Participatory Politics

Beam, George and Dick Simpson. *Strategies For Change.* Forthcoming, 1972.

This book will attempt to set forth alternative strategies for change by citizen participation in elections, by pressure tactics, and by attempts to initiate change within administrative structures. A basic thesis is that there is not a single successful strategy but that multiple strategies applied simultaneously and strategically may well bring political reform.

Harrington, Michael. *Toward a Democratic Left.* Baltimore: Penguin, 1969.

Harrington sees the primary need of the future to be the formation of a new coalition between the poor, the working class unions, youth, and professionals. This coalition, he believes, would best be formed within the current Democratic Party which would allow for changes in government policy through democratic means.

Kaufman, Arnold. *The Radical Liberal.* New York: Simon and Schuster, 1970. First published by Atherton, 1968.

Kaufman, without suggesting specific mechanisms for effectuating it, discusses a more radical form of liberalism which has faith in the potentialities of American democracy, is passionately moral but coldly calculating and energetic in the pursuit of its goals. In general, the goals of the radical liberal are to attained through constant and unremitting pressure.

Lowi, Theodore. *The End of Liberalism.* New York: Norton, 1969.
An analysis of the liberal or bureaucratic state, *The End of Liberalism* is concerned with how interest-group liberalism has created government programs which completely fail to get at the root of current problems. Instead of liberalism, Lowi calls for "juridical democracy." Before progress in solving problems can be made, we must first be motivated by the goal of justice, create a truly independent senior Civil Service, and formal mechanisms for administrative rule-making.

Wilson, James Q. *The Amateur Democrat.* Chicago: University of Chicago Press, 1962.
This study of amateur politicians and the political club movement in Chicago, Los Angeles, and New York provides one of the few critical analyses of the philosophy of amateur or participatory politics as well as the weaknesses of many of the reform organizations. It should be required reading for all who would venture to attempt political reforms related to issue-oriented or volunteer-based politics.

Index